Managing Quality in Schools

SCHOOL LEADERSHIP AND MANAGEMENT SERIES

Series Editors: Brent Davies and John West-Burnham

Other titles in the series:

Effective Learning in Schools
by Christopher Bowring-Carr and John West-Burnham

Middle Management in Schools
by Sonia Blandford

Reengineering and Total Quality in Schools
by Brent Davies and John West-Burnham

Resource Management in Schools
by Sonia Blandford

Strategic Marketing for Schools
by Brent Davies and Linda Ellison

Forthcoming titles:

Human Resource Management for Effective Schools
by John O'Neill and John West-Burnham

Leadership and Professional Development
by John West-Burnham

Strategic Direction and Development in Schools
by Brent Davies and Linda Ellison

Managing Quality in Schools

Second Edition

■ ■ ■

Effective Strategies for Quality-based School Improvement

JOHN WEST-BURNHAM

London · Hong Kong · Johannesburg · Melbourne · Singapore · Washington DC

For Daniel

PITMAN PUBLISHING
128 Long Acre, London WC2E 9AN
Tel: +44 (0) 171 447 2000
Fax: +44 (0) 171 240 5771

A Division of Pearson Professional Limited

First Edition published by Longman Group UK Limited in 1992
Second Edition published in Great Britain in 1997

© Longman Group UK Limited 1992
© Pearson Professional Limited 1997

The right of John West-Burnham to be identified as author of this work
has been asserted by him in accordance with the Copyright, Designs
and Patents Act 1988.

ISBN 0 273 62407 5

British Library Cataloguing in Publication Data
A CIP catalogue record for this book can be obtained from the British Library

10 9 8 7 6 5 4 3 2 1

Typeset by Phoenix Photosetting, Chatham, Kent
Printed and bound in Great Britain by Redwood Books, Trowbridge, Wiltshire

The Publishers' policy is to use paper manufactured from sustainable forests.

Contents

■　■　■

Preface to the Second Edition

■ ■ ■

I am very grateful to Pitman Publishing for commissioning a second edition of 'Managing Quality in Schools'. The publication of the first edition had far greater impact on my life than I could have ever imagined. What started as intellectual curiosity has resulted in five years of professional activity, new contacts and friendships and opportunities to be involved in wonderful projects in schools and the education service.

In the second edition I have sought to reflect changes in my own thinking over five years and to incorporate the ideas and most importantly the experience of others. My own understanding of total quality in education has been enriched by contact with an enormous range of people. Many of them are anonymous, teachers who came on courses and shared experiences. Many schools have allowed me to present ideas, some of which, hopefully, have led to practical improvements.

There are many people who through friendship and professional debate have kept my thinking alive and focused. Any list is unsatisfactory but a number deserves recognition: Christopher Bowring-Carr; Brent Davies; John Marsh; Ian McKenzie; Alan Murphy; Mike Pupius; Charles Sisum and Claire Trott as well as colleagues in Cheshire LEA; the Education Management Development Unit, University of Leicester and the International Educational Leadership Centre, Lincoln University campus.

Maureen Young managed production of the manuscript in an exemplary fashion and Michelle Darraugh and Anna Freeman of Pitman Publishing proved the most tolerant of publishers.

Finally, my love and thanks to Phyllis West-Burnham for her insights and wisdom. The first edition was dedicated to my son Daniel – he is still the inspiration for what education could and should be.

John West-Burnham

Introduction to the First Edition

■   ■   ■

The issues of quality and service are the major management concerns for all organisations in the 1990s. Industry and commerce in Britain have already started addressing them and awareness is increasing in the public sector, notably the NHS and local government.

This book assimilates and applies the lessons of the quality movement to schools. There is little in the book that is unique, it is rather a starting point, a contribution to the debate on how to ensure that schools provide the best possible learning opportunities for children. It is recognised that changes in the terminology of many of the chapters of this book would allow schools to claim that they already operate total quality management. This is not a problem. In fact it is essential that education does evolve its own view on how to manage quality.

Inevitably a book of this length can only highlight issues, but in doing so can demonstrate a contribution to the process of continuous improvement. It is very much hoped that readers will respond in the invitation in the review section in order to advance the debate.

A wide range of individuals and organisations have contributed, knowingly and unknowingly, to the writing of this book. To Joss and Daniel, for the loss of evenings and weekends, I give my love and thanks. Pat and Dave Lambert, Lyn Lambert and Jack Lindstrom provided quality thinking time, space and ideas. Kim Lewis of Ad hoc Systems Limited, Nottingham, displayed an amazing ability to get it right first time and Roger Henwood of Longman proved the most tolerant of customers.

Specific thanks must go to CRAC for organising the first significant course on TQM in education; to Jeff Prest of ICI, John Chesterton of ICL, Nick Massey of the Co-operative Bank, Steve Hart of Profile Consulting and John Woodward of Q.Ed., all of whom gave freely of ideas and time. Steve Holman first introduced me to the concepts of TQM. To all I send my thanks and the hope that I have done them justice.

Finally I acknowledge the many colleagues in Cheshire who have participated enthusiastically in courses where many of the ideas in this book have been explored and developed. They receive my special thanks and the reassurance that the final responsibility is mine and mine alone. Equally the views expressed here are mine.

John West-Burnham

1
■ ■ ■
Why Quality?

Introduction

This chapter seeks to set the debate about quality in schools in context, and to outline the particular approach adopted in this book. The fundamental assumption is that the changes facing schools following the 1988 Education Reform Act are so profound that traditional approaches to managing schools may no longer be appropriate and radical alternatives have to be considered. This chapter therefore explores:

- the changing context of school management;
- the drive for quality;
- total quality management;
- objections to the total quality approach;
- parallel developments.

The changing context of school management

Although schools have had to respond to a wide range of specific legislative changes it is the broader thematic issues that probably represent the greatest challenges to the prevailing view as to what constitutes an appropriate model for school management. As Drucker (1993) puts it:

> As knowledge becomes the resource of post-capitalist society, the social position of the school as 'producer' and 'distributive channel' of knowledge, and its monopoly, are both bound to be challenged. And some of the competitors are bound to succeed. . . . Indeed, no other institution faces challenges as radical as those that will transform the school. (p. 209)

Writing in 1995 Drucker agreed that in order to respond to profound social changes 'we will have to learn to define the *quality* of education and the productivity of education' and that 'we need systematic work on the quality of knowledge'. (p. 237)

What is clear is that existing models, mindscapes and conceptualisation of school management will become increasingly dysfunctional as the pace of social, technological and economic change intensifies. The issue is not just that what schools will have to manage is changing but how they will be able to manage is also changing. The demands are increasing and the resource base is diminishing. Caldwell (1997) argues that there are three parallel tracks influencing the reform of school education.

- **Track 1**. Creating systems of self-managing schools in the public sector (time horizon five years).
- **Track 2**. Unrelenting focus on restructuring learning and teaching in all schools (time horizon ten years).
- **Track 3**. Reengineering school education: a Gestalt for schooling for the knowledge society (time horizon 25 years).

In England and Wales track 1 is virtually completed, track 2 is just beginning to impact and track 3 is, for most educational professionals, a dream or, more exactly, a nightmare. The inescapable conclusion is that these tracks pose the greatest challenge to the existing orthodoxy, derived as it is from notions of organisational design that are essentially 19th century in origin. There is nothing intrinsically wrong with this – it seems to work very well for the Civil Service, the Armed Forces and other monolithic organisations. Whether in fact it is valid for a period of profound social change (as per Drucker) and appropriate for organisations primarily concerned with the learning of young people is a moot point.

It is difficult to be precise about the practical and specific changes that will occur but some of the key trends are:

- the increasing impact of information technology on learning and the nature of organisations (the virtual school?);
- an increasing emphasis on international perspectives;
- the movement towards the vertical integration of education, pre-school to higher education 'under one roof';
- diminishing public funding;
- rethinking of the role, status and deployment of education professionals;
- the insistent requirement for 'value for money'.

The cumulative impact of these changes may impose an impossible burden on schools in which the structure, organisation and care functions are rooted in an essentially static model of management. The impact of externally driven change requires a fundamental reorientation in the conceptualisation of what school management means. The changes that are known about have already proved profound in their effect.

The Education Acts of the 1980s and 1990s provide the most fundamental challenge to the established ways of doing things in schools. The changes are so basic it is doubtful that schools will survive unless their response to the changes is of the same order of magnitude as the changes themselves. Historically schools have responded to change in an incremental and piecemeal fashion, gradually assimilating some new requirements, subverting or modifying others and even ignoring a few. The realignment of the education service following the 1988 Education Act in particular makes such responses inappropriate and impractical. Indeed the lack of a co-ordinated response may well prove to be dysfunctional not only generating acute internal tensions but questioning the survival of the school itself. An analogy may be drawn with the person planning to take up the game of squash: investing in designer clothing and equipment, reading the rule book and joining the club but not bothering to develop the skills or, crucially, to get fit – a heart attack may result. In order to get fit a diagnosis of the demands to be made on the system is necessary.

Readers will not need reminding of the range and complexity of the changes impinging on schools. It is worth, however, itemising those components which pose the greatest challenge to established ways of working, summarised as: the National Curriculum, local management of schools, inspection, consumer rights and social pressures.

The National Curriculum

The key management issues may be identified as:

- managing time so as to meet all the requirements of the curriculum;
- developing resources in response to new demands;
- deploying staff to maximise available expertise;
- managing assessment procedures and recording achievement;
- developing staff in the new skills and knowledge;
- managing cross-curricular themes;
- implementing appropriate learning strategies;
- reporting academic outcomes;
- increasing emphasis on outcomes;
- publication of results in league tables.

Apart from these specific aspects the implications of the changes also have to be managed. Most significant of these are the demands on teacher time, e.g. the introduction of 'new' subjects and approaches to assessment in the primary school and the challenge to traditional ways of structuring learning in the secondary school. To the operational issues, therefore, must be added concerns about teacher stress, motivation and perceived challenges to traditional views of professional autonomy.

Local management of schools (LMS)

The impact and implications of LMS are increasingly understood and the specific issues may be identified as:

- the changing role of the governing body;
- integrating budgeting, curriculum and staffing plans into a strategic approach;
- managing parental choice procedures;
- assuming full responsibility for staffing;
- establishing administrative procedures;
- marketing the school;
- responding to new reporting, inspection and audit requirements;
- reviewing senior management roles and responsibilities;
- managing a formula-funded budget.

These factors have had the combined effect of requiring the implementation of a whole new range of procedures while potentially detracting from the core purpose of schools – the management of learning. They have confronted senior staff with stark choices and direct accountability for the implications of their actions. Issues related to job security and resource availability are now located directly in the school.

Inspection

The introduction of the OFSTED inspection process has been one of the most significant changes in the conceptualisation of the status of schools in society. The implications include:

- changing notions of accountability and answerability;
- public definitions of effectiveness and 'value for money';
- increasing public access to information;
- publication of criteria;
- development of reporting and planning;
- the impact on schools relative to the perceived benefits.

Fundamental to the inspection process is the issue of the validity of inspection itself, the cost effectiveness of the actual process, the integrity of the criteria applied and the demonstrable impact on school improvement.

Consumer rights

The introduction of a crypto-consumerism under LMS is likely to become more overt in response to citizens' and parents' charters. Possible implications of this approach might include:

- financial penalties and rewards linked to performance;
- increased demands for information;
- publication of comparative data;
- greater accessibility to school procedures.

Few teachers will object in principle to the notion that their customers should have the same rights as they enjoy as consumers. However, there is a substantial difference between complaining about a badly serviced car and complaints about literacy rates or GCSE results. The principle is the same but the measures to be applied and the variables operating are very different.

Social pressures

This is the least tangible of the factors impinging on school management in the 1990s but will be a vital determinant of quality. Unemployment, social disadvantage, domestic stress and cultural deprivation are all issues that act as crucial determinants on the ways in which schools are managed. The more acute the problems of the environment in which a school has to function the greater the demands on the skills and qualities of teachers and the fewer the resources likely to be available. If the factors outlined earlier are added to the social pressures under which many schools operate then the challenge to leaders and managers is profound.

To these pressures must be added increased competition between LEA maintained schools, the independent sector, grant maintained schools and city technology colleges. The equation is further complicated by changes in 16–19 provision and higher education as well as changes in the expectations of employers.

The combination of these factors poses the most significant challenge to the prevailing orthodoxies of the theory and practice of school management. The first response is that schools have to be managed by professionals who have the knowledge, skills and qualities appropriate to the new situation. Schools that deny the importance of planning, budget management and the deployment and development of staff in the context of curriculum leadership are putting a question mark over their survival. There is a need to develop a coherent and systematic view of what the management of learning in schools means. Symptomatic of the problem are the following aspects of school management:

- no clear or agreed criteria as to the components of school management;
- unclear definitions of the purpose of senior and middle management;
- deference to experience over skills and qualities;
- limited access to management – the word is used as a collective noun rather than to describe a process;
- training is often random, ad hoc and peripheral;
- administrative procedures are seen as a substitute for effective management;
- management as a process lacks a focus on learning.

The net effect of these elements is the danger that managerialism, i.e. procedures carried out for their own sake, will come to be regarded as managing. This will inevitably detract from the key purpose of schools and elevate concern for power, status and systems to the detriment of facilitating effective learning. Bureaucratic responses to the complexity are always the easiest. This problem is not unique to the education service. Many commercial, industrial and public sector organisations are facing a choice in responding to complex change: either become more formal and structured or adopt a radical and fundamental alternative. For many that alternative is total quality management.

The drive for quality

For the cynical, quality is the management 'flavour of the decade', a fashion, a bandwagon which in time will be replaced by another set of prescriptions. Formulations as to the 'correct approaches' undoubtedly change but it is possible to be more confident about the quality movement for two reasons. First, it has been around for 40 years – it is not a passing whim, it has taken a long time to percolate through the literature. Second, however quality is defined, it has always been at the centre of the debate about education. There are few other social processes where a concern for standards has been such a constant imperative. As has already been argued, the 1988 Education Reform Act highlights and reinforces this concern – to this must be added a range of other driving forces. Sallis (1996) has identified four imperatives for introducing total quality management (TQM): the professional, the moral, the competitive and survival. These he identified in the context of further education, but they are equally valid for schools. Changing the language to match the situation facing schools the reasons for adopting a quality management approach may be identified as moral, environmental, survival and accountability.

The moral imperative

If schools are about anything then they have to be fundamentally and obsessively concerned with providing children with the very best educational possibilities. It is difficult to conceptualise a situation where anything less than total quality is perceived as being appropriate or acceptable for the education of children. The moral imperative is concerned with optimising the opportunities for children to achieve their full potential so that their years of compulsory education culminate in the maximum appropriate outcomes. This places an enormous burden of responsibility on teachers and managers in schools to enhance every opportunity for the growth and development of children. This in turn requires that values are at the core of every decision-making process and educational procedure.

The moral imperative is very closely related to the professional imperative in that professionalism implies commitment to the needs of a client and an obligation to meet those needs by deploying knowledge and skills to best effect. Being a professional confers a moral imperative to deliver consistent, high levels of service. Crucially this applies as much to managing the school as to managing the classroom.

The environmental imperative

Schools are in a dynamic interaction with the society and community they serve. That environment is becoming increasingly quality conscious. If schools are to be genuinely responsive then they need increasingly to be aware of, and to respond to quality issues. Further and higher education, employers and other external agencies are using the vocabulary and processes of quality. Pupils leaving schools will go to work in TQM businesses, continue their studies in colleges with quality systems and, most importantly, go home to parents who are increasingly aware of their rights as citizens and consumers. Most schools have as part of their aims the 'preparation of pupils for work, continuing education and citizenship'. If this is to be a genuine experience rather than didactic imperative schools will need to assimilate the vocabulary and processes of quality.

Just as significant is the fact that as schools become increasingly autonomous in their dealings with external agencies, suppliers etc., so they should become more articulate in demanding quality service.

The survival imperative

The pressures of LMS raise the very real possibilities of compulsory redundancy and school closures. In simplistic terms enrolments will fall and schools will cease to be viable if they fail to satisfy customer needs and expectations. The customer-driven approach of TQM is therefore a pragmatic response to ensuring continuing recruitment of pupils.

However, this does not imply a desperate attempt at cloning that which is perceived to be 'best school', rather a genuine responsiveness to the specific community in which a school is located. One of the imperatives facing senior managers in schools is the survival of the school – parental satisfaction is one of the key determinants of a school's viability. TQM provides a powerful mechanism for ensuring consistency of response.

The accountability imperative

The increasing emphasis on the inspection and reporting of schools requires the development of internal strategies to generate appropriate data and processes which will accommodate and incorporate reporting and inspection procedures. TQM provides the vehicle for making these procedures intrinsic to school management processes and ensuring effective response. If reporting and inspection are seen as ways of responding to customer requirements then they will become implicit to school processes rather than an 'alien' activity.

The net results of these imperatives is that schools will have to see themselves as part of their communities, not in the sense of identifying and providing services they consider appropriate but rather in meeting the needs and requirements as specified by that community. Total quality management provides an integrated response which has the potential to meet the demands of these imperatives in a manner which is consistent with the special nature of schools as organisations.

Total quality management

Detailed definitions of TQM are developed in Chapter 2 and applied throughout the rest of this book. However, it is appropriate at this stage to introduce its key components to demonstrate how it meets the needs identified so far in this chapter. The key principles of TQM may be summarised as shown in Figure 1.1.

These basic points are elaborated throughout this book, but it is worth stressing at this stage that TQM organisations are about much more than responding to clients. They are as much about creativity, team work, celebration, growth, recognition and excitement as creating effective processes, which is why this

FOCUS	Internal and external customers
DEFINITION	Meeting customer requirements
SCOPE	Every aspect of the organisation
RESPONSIBILITY	Everyone
STANDARD	Right First Time – fitness for purpose
METHOD	Prevention not detection
MEASUREMENT	Zero defects
CULTURE	Continuous improvement

Figure 1.1 Defining total quality management

book argues that TQM is particularly appropriate for schools. TQM will not work if it is perceived as a series of mechanistic processes. Above everything else it is about the quality of personal relationships and this is an area where schools should have a significant advantage.

Equally significantly TQM is about survival, it is a means for ensuring that a particular organisation is the natural 'first choice' for its potential customers. Every reader will be aware of having made deliberate choices to buy or not buy a particular product or service on the basis of personal satisfaction or dissatisfaction. The central determination in returning to a shop, a garage, a restaurant or holiday resort is most likely to be the extent to which needs were met and how they were met. The choices which teachers apply in their own social and economic lives are now available to their customers.

TQM therefore provides an approach to managing schools which is sufficiently pragmatic to meet the changing environment that schools are having to operate in while being centrally and fundamentally concerned with values and moral considerations. However, it would be naive to imagine that a system originated by American engineers and developed in Japanese mass production companies will automatically commend itself to British teachers.

There is a growing, if limited, body of experience to suggest that TQM does have much to offer schools.

> *What have we gained? At heart, a philosophy which suits our parents and our school. We have, as most outsiders note, a greater degree of internal consistency and coherence than most schools of our size. Above all, we have a mission statement which is not just a form of words, but a statement of our ethos and values which drive our development plan, our governors, staff, pupils and parents. (Samuel 1997, p. 107)*

Sisum (1997) identifies some of the outcomes and lessons from the adoption of a total quality approach in a school.

> *Planning processes for improvement is a relatively neglected area. Without the background to Quality Management principles and approaches we would have found it very difficult to manage the complexities of action planning. (p. 123)*

Hendry (1994) provides yet another insight.

> *We all feel that we have broadened our understanding of KSI assessment by taking a TQM approach. It has forced us to look much further afield than previously in our consideration of needs in the assessment process, and our aim in our quest for quality and continuous improvement is that every child in our care will benefit from a more tightly organised and monitored establishment. (p. 35)*

Healy (1994) shows how the introduction of quality techniques can lead to profound changes in a school.

> *Quality is dynamic, it never stays the same. We have identified five issues which will form the focus of our next development phase:*
>
> - *reinforce autonomy in team working*
> - *remove the hierarchical structure through the introduction of a flatter management structure*
> - *reorganise the school structure to reflect quality development*
> - *the introduction of quality managers*
> - *delegating more of the financial budget to teams. (p. 68)*

The work of Parsons (1994), Doherty (1994), Lomax (1996) and Davies and West-Burnham (1997) provide abundant examples of successful attempts (although by no means unproblematic) to apply total quality principles to schools.

Of course there are many schools that are highly successful and have never even contemplated total quality as an option. Total quality is not proposed as a universal panacea to the exclusion of all others but rather an approach which may be right for some schools at a particular stage of their development. There appears to be a prima facie case that total quality may have validity in some educational contexts.

Objections to the total quality approach

Everard and Morris (1990) provide a useful and succinct summary of a number of objections to the notion of management in education. The objections are largely academic and in many cases have been overtaken by events, i.e. schools have to be managed in order to survive. However, pragmatism does not guarantee appropriate styles of management. The main objections may be summarised as follows:

1 Managerialism denies professionalism.
2 Hierarchical accountability diminishes collegiality and autonomy.
3 The emphasis on leadership denies democracy. //
4 Managerialism denies educational values.
5 Management is inevitably manipulative.
6 Educational outcomes cannot be managed.

It is difficult to respond to these concerns without challenging a fundamental misapprehension, i.e. the claimed definition of management. Many organisations would share the concerns just identified; most TQM companies would reject the implicit definitions of management as a power-based, coercive, manipulative strategy which is cynically pragmatic as inappropriate and unacceptable. It will be for the reader to decide at the end of this book if the six objections are valid with respect to TQM. A central hypothesis of this study is that TQM is an appropriate model for schools because it does counter each objection.

There is every good reason for rejecting managerialism, i.e. management for its own sake where systems, status and routines take priority over real needs. TQM offers a value-driven approach to management based on effective human relationships. While educational outcomes may be intangible educational processes are not – they are based on the reality of day-to-day interactions in classrooms and staffrooms and these have to be managed. What is undeniable is that many schools that would reject the conceptual framework of TQM do in fact practise quality management. The labels are less significant than the content. Equally there are other initiatives which parallel the TQM movement but which are particular to schools.

Lomax (1996) and her colleagues raise a number of significant concerns about the validity of quality approaches by arguing that they could be seen as pragmatic and reactive to imposed changes rather than a response based on

> *morally committed action which would emphasise a critical approach to practices seen to deny social justice rather than a blind acceptance of legislation and a technical response to it . . . (this is) to deplore the idea that quality management can only focus on the means and make little comment about ends. (p. 2)*

This is a fairly fundamental misapprehension about the nature of total quality as will be demonstrated in Chapter 2. The many concerns that have been raised about the appropriateness of total quality have usually been based on a limited view of quality – concentrating on aspects of quality assurance rather than the holistic model.

Two other concerns about the validity of total quality approaches are worth raising at this stage: first doubts about whether it actually works in the business sector. The Japanese economic miracle appears to have stumbled in its inexorable march, many organisations espousing total quality have failed and about 70 per cent of total quality initiatives in business apparently fail. There does appear to be a consensus that failure results from not implementing total quality *totally*. Any philosophy will be compromised if it is not fully expressed. It is also the case that in a dynamic environment the philosophy needs to evolve to take into account new and unforeseen challenges and demands. It is probably true to say that businesses that have adopted a quality approach have done better than those that have not.

Second is the issue as to the extent to which total quality is sufficiently radical to meet the challenges facing organisations of all types. Davies (Davies and Ellison, 1997, p. 12) has argued for the need to reengineer education which involves:

> radical redesign to achieve dramatic improvements. 'Radical' is defined as 'going to the root of things' and is a zero-based approach to find and treat causes of organisational ineffectiveness and not merely to treat the symptoms. 'Redesign' is where the old is thrown away and individuals start with the proverbial 'clean sheet'.

There is much in the reengineering approach in terms of the mindset necessary to 'break the mould'. Total quality offers an approach to sustain that mindset and provides the practical roots to allow the process to take place.

Parallel developments

Two main initiatives may be identified which have the same concerns and many of the same outcomes as TQM: the 'effective schools' movement and school improvement. The research into effective schools has been usefully distilled by Hopkins (1987, p. 3) where he identifies eight organisational factors characteristic of effective schools.

1 Curriculum-focused leadership.
2 Supportive climate.
3 Emphasis on learning.
4 Clear goals and high expectations.
5 Monitoring performance and achievement.
6 Continuous staff development.

7   Parental involvement.

8   LEA support.

Hopkins also stresses the importance of process factors in creating effective schools; quoting Fullan (1985) he identifies four factors:

1   Leadership as process rather than status.
2   An explicit value system which is consensual.
3   Sophisticated social interaction and communication.
4   Collaborative planning.

Slight changes in language and emphasis would allow these factors to be claimed by many TQM companies. The issue that is frequently not addressed in the educational literature is how to achieve these situations in practical terms.

The International School Improvement Project (ISIP) produced an important international perspective on the issues relevant to school improvement and from the report it published a number of 'lessons' for schools in the UK emerged.

1   Careful and accurate situational analysis.
2   Needs carefully identified.
3   Need for change clearly appreciated.
4   Carefully thought-out strategy.
5   Strategy communicated effectively.
6   Changes reinforced and institutionalised.
7   Changes supported and resourced.

(Hopkins 1987, p. 188).

The parallels with the principles for effectiveness and the definition of TQM in Figure 1.1 are clear. The links are reinforced in Chapter 9, most importantly in the notion of continuous improvement through development. Although its cultural pedigree is very different, TQM has many significant parallels with existing initiatives in education. What TQM has to offer is an holistic approach; an integrated view which incorporates structures, processes and relationships. However, there is no 'off the shelf package', no neat series of prescriptions. Although many TQM organisations have approaches in common and use similar language, the actual operation of TQM has to be unique; it must be created by the school in response to its own environment and through its own processes.

Summary

- The complexity of the changes facing schools requires radical changes to management styles.
- The key demands on schools may be identified as the National Curriculum, LMS, inspection, consumer rights and social pressures.
- Traditional approaches to education management may no longer be appropriate.
- Quality is an increasingly significant issue for all organisations in Britain.
- Total quality management offers an appropriate response to the demands on schools and the need for a new management approach.
- The objections to management in schools are based on fundamental misapprehensions.
- TQM is compatible with other educational initiatives concerned with effectiveness and improvement.

Action

Establish the extent to which you are working in a quality school by completing the following review. Compare your perception with that of your colleagues.

1 What is the moral and philosophical basis for management in your school?

2 To what extent are management processes derived from and consistent with the core purpose of the school?

3 What is the rationale for the way in which your school is structured?

4 How close is the correlation between your intentions as a school (e.g. aims) and the actual experience of pupils, parents, staff etc.?

5 When was the last time that the philosophy, structure and working processes of the school were subject to a fundamental review?

6 How strong is the consensus about the validity and integrity of school management structures?

7 How confident are you that existing patterns of school organisation are appropriate for the changes facing education?

8 Does school management take up a disproportionate amount of time?

2

■ ■ ■

Defining Quality

Introduction

The innocent reader approaching the topic of total quality management is likely to be overwhelmed by the range of (often contradictory) advice available. The literature on quality covers the spectrum from the highly technical, mathematically inspired texts through academic discourse to the frankly anecdotal 'I did it my way – you can do it too' memoirs of captains of industry. The purpose of this chapter is to try to disentangle those elements that are most useful to managers in schools and propose a definition of total quality that is applicable to the education service.

This chapter examines the following aspects of the quality debate:

- the evolution of total quality;
- clarification of key concepts;
- the quality 'gurus';
- TQM in practice;
- the debate on 'excellence';
- quality in school management.

The evolution of total quality

Total quality management emerged in Japan in the years following World War II. Paradoxically the movement was inspired and sustained by two Americans, Deming and Juran. Their early work was largely concerned with statistical methods of measuring quality in the engineering industry. During the 1950s and 1960s the purely statistical approach was extended and developed by Deming and Juran and increasingly by Japanese industrialists and management writers, notably Ishikawa and Taguchi. The success of many

Japanese industries in the 1960s and 1970s has been very largely credited to the quality movement. Most British homes will bear testimony to the success of the Japanese electronic industry. Virtually every British school will possess a Japanese photocopier and video player and will depend on Japanese microchips. Many British school children will watch too much TV on Japanese televisions and many sixteen year old students will aspire to own a Japanese motorbike. The lessons of quality management are already available to schools.

It would be inappropriate and foolish to propose that what worked for Japanese industry is appropriate for British industry, let alone British schools. Several writers have already pointed out that the success of Japan was due as much to national culture as to management theory. However, in the late 1970s the work of Deming in particular was 'discovered' in the USA and this led to an explosion of activity in American industry with Crosby emerging as the most influential 'evangelist'. At about the same time Peters and Waterman published *In Search of Excellence* (1982) which worked from a different set of premises but reinforced the fundamental message that explains the success of the Japanese – customer satisfaction is everything.

This message began to make an impact in Britain in the early 1980s and there has been a number of significant initiatives, notably the National Quality Campaign, the establishment of the British Quality Association in 1981 and the government White paper 'Standards, Quality and International Competitiveness' published in 1982. It is difficult, if not impossible, to quantify the impact of the quality movement on British industry, commerce and the public sector. There is evidence of increasing interest by virtue of the volume of training and consultancy taking place, the demand for BS5750 accreditation, the job advertisements for quality managers and the number of organisations using a concept of quality in their corporate image. 1991 saw a significant awakening of interest in the education sector, notably in LEAs, higher and further education.

What has emerged in the 1990s is an increasing confidence in organisations that they do not need to adopt specific formulations but rather should adapt the principles of TQM to suit their own needs and principles. One of the most significant changes has been the emergence of total quality as opposed to TQM. The problem was with the 'M'. Management has evolved a much more specific definition which helps to contextualise it and differentiate a range of functions. Most important is the increasing emphasis and recognition of the significance of what might be described as 'higher order' activities, notably the importance attached to vision, values, leadership and strategic thinking.

Organisations have modified the language of total quality to the point where it would need a genealogist to establish the pedigree of their management culture. This is a healthy development which indicates the strength of the underlying principles of Deming and his fellow originators. The philosophy of total quality has matured and been applied in a wide range of contexts and the language used to describe it has been modified to meet specific needs.

Clarification of key concepts

Few concepts are as open to abuse as 'quality'. It is a universal panacea for organisational ills, an incontrovertible imperative and a reassuring message to clients – few will deny that they accept the value of 'quality'. The first crucial issue is to see management for quality as a process rather than a product. One of the major problems in the educational service is that the achievement of quality is perceived as an intellectual problem rather than a management process. In this sense quality management becomes a search after a Platonic absolute rather than an Aristotelian analysis of action to be taken. Quality has to be seen in terms of relationships rather than intangible (and unattainable) goals. To see quality as an elusive abstract is to deny the possibility of its attainment and so justify a power-based, controlling relationship. If quality is defined by clients in terms of relationships then it becomes potentially attainable.

The status of the concept of quality largely determines the management behaviour it generates. This is best exemplified in the uncertain and often ambiguous use of the terms inspection, quality control, quality assurance and quality management. It is very important to adopt sharp definitions of these terms as the implications of each are very different. The relationship between these elements and their associated levels of management sophistication is shown in Figure 2.1.

As an organisation moves from inspection to quality management so a number of significant culture changes take place:

- there is increasing awareness and involvement of clients and suppliers;
- personal responsibility of the work force increases;
- there is increasing emphasis on process as well as product;
- the imperative is towards continuous improvement.

Fundamental to the transformation is the relationship of costs to product. Inspection might detect a 20 per cent failure rate and this might be a cause for congratulations. However, the questions remain: Did the system detect all failures? Were the criteria for failure acceptable to customers? What is the impact on workers of having one-fifth of the output rejected? In essence if an inspection system rejects 20 per cent then the work force is being paid to produce rubbish on one day each week.

TOTAL QUALITY MANAGEMENT	INVOLVES SUPPLIERS AND CUSTOMERS AIMS FOR CONTINUOUS IMPROVEMENT CONCERNS PRODUCTS AND PROCESSES RESPONSIBILITY WITH ALL WORKERS DELIVERED THROUGH TEAM WORK
QUALITY ASSURANCE	USE OF STATISTICAL PROCESS CONTROL EMPHASIS ON PREVENTION EXTERNAL ACCREDITATION DELEGATED INVOLVEMENT AUDIT OF QUALITY SYSTEMS CAUSE AND EFFECTS ANALYSIS
QUALITY CONTROL	CONCERNED WITH PRODUCT TESTING RESPONSIBILITY WITH SUPERVISORS LIMITED QUALITY CRITERIA SOME SELF-INSPECTION PAPER-BASED SYSTEMS
INSPECTION	POST PRODUCTION REVIEW REWORKING REJECTION CONTROL OF WORK FORCE LIMITED TO PHYSICAL PRODUCTS

Figure 2.1 The hierarchy of quality management
(*Source*: derived from Dale and Plunkett 1990, p. 4)

This issue is at the heart of the quality movement. If quality is delivered as a remote absolute then it becomes possible to tolerate failure. Indeed failure is seen as confirmation of just how significant the definition is. A hierarchical definition of quality will always create an acceptance of failure and a justification for designing processes that are actually posited on a significant proportion of those involved in it failing. This is most powerfully exemplified in the response of some to recent improvements in GCSE and A level examination results. If fewer are failing then standards must be slipping. This is the tyranny of the bell curve, the notion that there has to be a 'normal' distribution curve.

Few of those who argue for the maintenance of standards based on a distribution curve would accept such a model in any other aspect of their lives, yet are robust to the point of dogmatism that it is impossible for all children to succeed.

The quality 'gurus'

This section will introduce briefly the key components of the theories of the quality gurus. All are prolific in their writing and their messages are not consistent; indeed there are somewhat Byzantine ideological disputes between their adherents. The amount of contradictory advice may well induce the well known 'paralysis by analysis' syndrome. It is not proposed to offer systematic comparative review but rather highlight the key components of each writer's thinking.

Crosby

Philip Crosby is probably the most significant writer in terms of influence in the USA and Europe. He focuses on senior management and argues the centrality of increased profitability through quality improvement. He is best known for his four absolutes of quality management:

1	The definition	Quality is conformance to customer requirements, not intrinsic goodness.
2	The system	Prevention, not detection.
3	The standard	Zero defects.
4	The measurement	The price of non-conformance.

These absolutes have been adopted by many companies and have almost become synonymous with TQM. Their relevance to schools will be discussed later but it would be wrong to pretend that they are unproblematic in any context. In particular it is argued that zero defects as a performance standard is hopelessly unrealistic. However, the conceptual framework the absolutes offer do help to distinguish TQM from other management approaches. Equally useful are Crosby's fourteen steps to quality improvement – the basis for implementation in many companies.

Crosby's fourteen steps

Step 1   Establish full management commitment to the quality programme.

Step 2   Set up a quality team to drive the programme.

Step 3   Introduce quality measurement procedures.

Step 4   Define and apply the principle of the cost of quality.

Step 5   Institute a quality awareness programme.

Step 6   Introduce corrective action procedures.

Step 7   Plan for the implementation of zero defects.

Step 8   Implement supervisor training.

Step 9   Announce zero defects day to launch the process.

Step 10   Set goals to bring about action.

Step 11   Set up employee–management communications systems.

Step 12   Recognise those who have actively participated.

Step 13   Set up quality councils to sustain the process.

Step 14   Do it all over again.

These steps have been criticised as being too (doctrinaire) and not always appropriate to different company cultures.

Deming

W. Edwards Deming's approach to quality management is derived from statistical methodologies. Deming advocates the use of statistical methods to reduce variability and so improve production. He argues that 85 per cent of production faults are the responsibility of management not employees. Inspection is inappropriate because it is post-facto, usually ineffective and costly. Instead he proposes an emphasis on precision, performance and attention to customers' requirements; for Deming this is best done through statistical methods designed to reduce variation. Like Crosby, Deming has synthesised his views on quality management into fourteen points:

Deming's fourteen points for management

Point 1   Create constancy of purpose for continual improvement of products and services.

Point 2   Adopt the new philosophy and abandon traditional ways of working.

Point 3   Move from inspection to building quality into every product and process.

Point 4   Stop awarding contracts on the basis of lowest bid – specify and buy quality.

Point 5   Engage in a process of continually improving every aspect of company activity.

Point 6   Use work-based training techniques.

Point 7   The emphasis for leaders and managers must be on quality, not quantity.

Point 8   Drive out fear by improving communication.

Point 9   Break down organisation barriers.

Point 10   Eliminate slogans and exhortations.

Point 11   Eliminate arbitrary numerical targets.

Point 12   Allow for pride of workmanship by locating responsibility with the worker.

Point 13   Encourage education and self-development.

Point 14   Create a management structure and culture that will drive the preceding 13 points.

Deming has been criticised for the perceived banality of these points. His philosophy has, however, been widely adopted and applied and is highly congruent with that of other theorists.

Juran

Joseph Juran is generally recognised as the most intellectually profound of the management theorists. Juran defines quality as 'fitness for purpose' and identifies the principal outcome of quality management as reducing the cost of quality and increasing conformance. He identifies three steps to quality improvement:

1   Structural annual improvement plans.
2   Training for the whole organisation.
3   Quality directed leadership.

Juran identifies the following components of a systematic approach to a company-wide quality programme:

1   Identify goals and policies for quality.
2   Implement plans to meet the goals.
3   Provide resources to evaluate progress.
4   Ensure appropriate motivation.

As with other 'gurus' Juran has summarised his principles of quality management into a series of epithets.

Juran's ten steps to quality improvement

Step 1   Create awareness of the need and opportunity for improvement.

Step 2   Set explicit goals for improvement.

Step 3   Create an organisational structure to drive the improvement process.

Step 4   Provide appropriate training.

Step 5   Adopt a project approach to problem solving.

Step 6   Identify and report progress.

Step 7   Recognise and reinforce success.

Step 8   Communicate results.

Step 9   Keep records of change.

Step 10   Build an annual improvement cycle into all company processes.

Juran places great emphasis on leadership and team work arguing that quality management is a balance of human relations skills and statistical process control skills.

Crosby, Deming and Juran may be safely credited with creating the vocabulary of total quality management although there are significant differences between them. There is a substantial number of other theorists and a rapidly increasing number of commentators. Feigenbaum is noteworthy in that he is generally credited with linking 'total' and 'quality'. His approach is technical and highly detailed but he does stress the importance of quality approaches permeating every aspect of an organisation.

Conway (as cited in MacDonald and Piggott 1990) stresses the importance of total quality management as a process rather than an objective, and proposes six basic tools for quality improvement.

- human relation skills;
- statistical data collection;
- use of statistical display techniques to inform;
- statistical process control, measuring to reduce variation;
- imagineering – visualising an ideal state;
- organising work to facilitate improvement.

The Japanese influence on the West has been limited but is now increasing, particularly in the areas of implementation and the development of analytical techniques. The most significant contributors in this field are Kaoru Ishikawa and Genichi Taguchi.

Although it is easy to parody the differences between the gurus and become over-burdened by the sheer volume of advice and exhortation, all writers are practical exponents of their theories and they have made them work.

Of the quality gurus Deming has been the most influential in the education sector. The work of the British Deming Association in particular has been highly influential in a significant number of schools and colleges. The school which pioneered total quality in education, Mt Edgecumbe High School in Sitka, Alaska, did so on the basis of Deming's fourteen points. A number of the most significant texts on quality in education have taken Deming as their starting-point. What is important is that in every case it has been necessary to interpret and apply Deming's principles – no theoretical construct can be applied without translation and interpretation.

Larrae Rocheleau, the late, much lamented Principal of Mt Edgecumbe modified the fourteen points into twelve of his own (as cited in Greenwood and Gaunt (1994) p. 14).

Point 1   Human relations are the foundation for all quality improvement.

Point 2   All components in our organisation can be improved.

Point 3   Removing the causes of problems in the system inevitably leads to improvement.

Point 4   The person doing the job is most knowledgeable about the job.

Point 5   People want to be involved and to do their jobs well.

Point 6   Every person wants to feel like a valued contributor.

Point 7   More can be accomplished by working together to improve the system than by working individually around the system.

Point 8   A structured problem-solving process using statistical graphic problem-solving techniques lets you know where you are, where the variations lie, the relative importance of the problems to be solved and whether the changes have had the desired impact.

Point 9   Adversarial relationships are counterproductive and outmoded.

Point 10   Every organisation has undiscovered gems waiting to be developed.

Point 11   Removing the barriers to pride of workmanship and joy of learning unlocks the true untapped potential of the organisation.

Point 12   Ongoing training, learning and experimentation is a priority for continuous improvement.

It has to be stressed that this is one view developed and applied in a particular school, although every report about Mt Edgecumbe indicates its distinctiveness and its success by a wide range of criteria.

One of the most useful current developments in the process of exchange between business and educational thinking is the cross-fertilisation of ideas around the European Foundation for Quality Management award (see Figure 2.2). Central to this work in Britain have been Charles Sisum, formerly a headteacher in Sheffield, and Mike Pupius of the Royal Mail. The following account of the application of the EFQM model to schools is by Sisum (1996).

During the school year 1994–95 I was granted leave of absence from my post of Headteacher at Wisewood School in Sheffield in order to take up a secondment as a Quality Manager within Royal Mail North East's Quality Directorate. The opportunity to experience a management role in an organisation as extensive and proactive in the field of continuous organisational improvement was an exciting prospect. It had been made possible by the Post Office's involvement in the prestigious Headteachers into Industry scheme based at the University of Warwick within which framework my secondment was placed, sponsored jointly by Royal Mail and Sheffield Training and Enterprise Council.

As my first year progressed I found myself immersed in the processes, language and general culture of Total Quality Management or as it is increasingly called, Business Excellence. My secondment induction programme led me through the world of Business Process Improvement (BPI) and the tools and techniques of facilitating such activity in the core functions of Royal Mail. As an extension to this work on quality improvement I became familiar with the model of Royal Mail's self-review process, known as Unit Excellence (Royal Mail, 1994) at the level of individual operational units, but when applied to the organisation at divisional level renamed Business Excellence Review (BER). The framework is a development of the European Foundation for Quality Management's self-review model (EFQM) for commercial organisations who wish to judge their progress down the 'quality road'. (Royal Mail 1995)

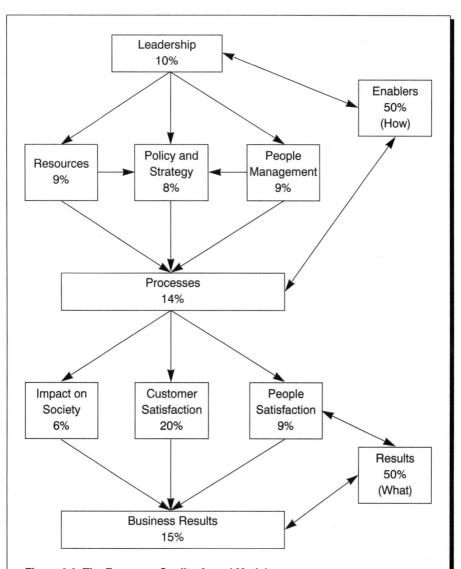

Figure 2.2 The European Quality Award Model
(Source: adapted from Royal Mail 1995)

The model suggests that organisations, however small or large, can be seen as being made up of a series of Enablers who, working through a series of Processes, are able to release the talents of the people in the organisation to produce a set of outcomes or Business Results. As the headteacher of a school shortly to go through the inspection experience, which is allegedly about the notion of school improvement, I became fascinated by the prospect that I might have stumbled across an alternative model of organisational improvement which was more developmental and involving for the school community than the quality control approach of the OFSTED Framework. (OFSTED 1995)

The basis of the EFQM self-review approach is one of critical self-analysis according to pre-set questions concerning the ways of working through the Processes identified with each Enabler box in the organisational model. To these are added critical questions relating to the measurement of improvement. At the Results end of the model the questions are focused on the Customers of the Enabler Processes as well as the pure Business Results and the Results box that attract questions concerning the measurement of Customer Satisfaction.

It is not difficult to see the similarity between the EFQM self-review organisational model and the notion of a school, working in a community and providing a service for the 'customers' known as pupils and parents. The internal customers of teaching and support staff not only appear on the Enabler side of the model in the People Management area but also on the Results side of the model in the People Satisfaction box. Business Results in a school setting may be defined in many ways using a variety of measures. Commonly it is the area of academic achievement that is the usual focus for attention but here again the model can be extended to other outcomes which those in the school may judge to be important. Levels of parent involvement, numbers of community partnerships or income from waste recycling are just three possible examples. Accordingly it is possible to translate the Enabler and Results criteria of the commercial world's EFQM model to language that is more appropriate to the fields of public service or not-for-profit organisations such as schools.

The exciting aspect of the EFQM self-review approach is that its method of application is based on the principles of TQM, i.e. the review process is carried out by the people who do the job, not imposed from outside the organisation, and yet it provides a framework for rigorous professional self-analysis which in turn can lead to the development of strategies for improvement in all areas of the organisation. When the review process is carried out on a regular basis such as a biennial cycle then the culture of continuous improvement has been born.

TQM in practice

It is not the purpose of this section to identify TQM companies and then exhort schools to do likewise – quite the reverse. The following examples are offered to demonstrate the practical realities of adopting a quality approach and to demonstrate a crucial fact – there are no 'off the shelf' solutions to the issue of quality.

Marks and Spencer

Perversely Marks and Spencer is not a TQM company, in that it has not followed or adopted the teachings of any of the American gurus. There is a very strong case for arguing that Sieff (1991) should be included in the pantheon of the quality 'greats'. Yet in many ways Marks and Spencer has been practising TQM for over half a century, and the company name is synonymous with quality in British retailing.

The company's image, status and success are founded on the simple principle of pleasing the customer by getting quality right first and then dealing with issues of price and returns. The company's motivation is primarily a moral one and this influences every facet of corporate culture and operating procedures. A number of very specific strategies can be identified:

- **Customer orientation:** This applies to product range, price and quality and to personal relationships, responses to complaints, the notion of customer entitlement and continual responsiveness.
- **Personnel issues:** Marks and Spencer is famous for its treatment of its staff, who are treated with trust and respect and work in a quality environment in terms of welfare, employment conditions and development.
- **Suppliers:** The company has long operated a quality relationship with its suppliers which works in two ways. First, Marks and Spencer is involved in every aspect of the production process; standards are published for raw materials and manufacturing processes; there is a certification process for suppliers and technical support to develop new products. Second, there are explicit expectations as to the nature of the relationship between supplier and customer.
- **Codifying procedures:** All procedures are standardised and documented for both internal operations and for suppliers. Operational simplicity is a driving force.
- **Benchmarking:** The company is constantly and acutely aware of the performance of competitors, analysing rival products and identifying areas for development. This process is reflected in the work of the technical departments which analyse every aspect of a product.

Perhaps the most significant feature of Marks and Spencer is the acute company-wide awareness of the need constantly to focus on quality. No organisation could possibly hope to replicate the Marks and Spencer approach by a process of duplication. With Marks and Spencer quality is not a 'what' or a 'how' but a 'why' – it is the *raison d'être* of the company.

As Bottery (1994) notes in his discussion of the lessons for education to be derived from Marks and Spencer:

> *Total quality control does not come through a myopic concentration upon attainment targets at 7, 11, 14 and 16. These should be the products of the system, not its objectives. Instead it comes by setting up the conditions for a high-quality delivery such that the attainment of these targets is a natural product of the system initiated.... M&S has already gone a long way in achieving such goals. The conception of such a system in education can be greatly helped by the example of organisational techniques and attitudes (in M&S). (p. 27)*

The National Trust

Webb (1991) argues that the National Trust is a classic example of how a service, i.e. non-profit organisation, can work towards quality. Webb argues that the criteria for quality in a service organisation are derived from the organisation's objectives, how well they are met and whether or not they conform with quality (p. 83). He argues that the NT meets its objectives in that it maximises access and conservation, increases its preservation work while respecting the interests of a wide range of pressure groups.

According to Webb the factors which lead to this perceived quality are:

- clarity and consistency of philosophy and strategy;
- clear decision-making;
- decentralised staff with a high degree of specialisation;
- clarity of communication channels;
- objective budgeting;
- clear delineations of policy-making, management and specialist functions;
- high motivation of full-time staff and volunteers.

Although the Trust is a unique organisation and it is difficult to extrapolate from it to the education service the related notions of clarity of purpose, relevant structure and effective communications are valid.

ICI

Every visitor to an ICI works is presented with a card outlining safety procedures; on the other side of the card is the simple message 'Safety first, quality second, profits third'. This exemplifies the philosophy of one of Britain's most consistently successful industrial concerns. The reasons for this success have been the subject of much debate and analysis, but Lessem (1985) advances the following:

1 A belief in the importance of the individual and that the organisation must be built around the individual.

2 An emphasis on the importance of corporate renewal constantly growing and evolving.

3 Integration of business, technological and personal development.

4 Leadership concerned with vision and enabling.

5 Creation of an open, collaborative culture.

6 An obsession with technical excellence, 'delighting the customer' with better quality, better value and innovative products.

Much has been made of the inspirational leadership of ICI by John Harvey-Jones, although he would minimise his personal impact. There is no doubt that quality companies have changed and developed through visionary leadership rather than dutiful role following.

It was not the intention of this section to offer paragons of virtue to be emulated, but rather to stress the importance of any organisation having a view of what it wants to be and how to achieve that vision. Crucial to the examples cited is the detailed extrapolation from principle into practice and, crucially, the importance of consistency in all processes. There are doubtless many schools and colleges which could legitimately claim inclusion in any listing of organisations driven by quality principles but the evidence is yet to be collected and codified.

Total quality in the public sector

Comparisons with business are usually helpful but problematic. Most commercial organisations would be delighted if their customers were required by law to use their services. However, the introduction of quality principles into the public sector does provide a bridge between purely for-profit organisations and those that, while increasingly operating in a commercial manner, do so in the context of public service. It is fair to say that all attempts in the public sector are constrained by political will. It is a moot point whether total quality is ever possible in a politically determined policy environment.

There are some useful examples of a move towards quality principles:

- Governmental bodies simplifying documentation to make it more user-friendly.
- The setting of performance targets, e.g. with road building and transport systems.
- Hospitals focusing on the individual in terms of information, appointment times, visiting arrangements etc.
- The movement from police forces to a police service.

- The emphasis in the former utilities on improving the quality of service through technological innovation.
- The work of the Royal Mail in setting performance targets for the delivery of services.

These examples are problematic as they occur in the context of privatisation and the opening up of many former monopolies to competition. However, they can be interpreted as an increasing recognition of consumer rights and an emphasis on service rather than on a bureaucratic management system.

The debate on 'excellence'

The excellence movement parallels the rise of total quality management in that both were initiated in the USA in the late 1970s. In 1980 Hayes and Abernathy published an article in the *Harvard Business Review* entitled 'Managing our way to economic decline'. The article was a searing indictment of the then prevalent management orthodoxy in the USA. They argued that the emergence of Japan as an economic superpower was primarily due to a failure of management rather than new factories and cheap labour in the Far East or problems with unions and government at home. The real problem was a lack of vision and leadership; American managers were preoccupied with a short-term financial approach to managing industry and commerce.

Peters and Waterman

In 1982 Peters and Waterman published *In Search of Excellence* which has sold five million copies worldwide. It built on the hypothesis advanced by Hayes and Abernathy and is generally credited with changing the prevailing management culture in the West. The book is essentially an analysis of what were recognised generally as successful companies. On the basis of this analysis Peters and Waterman extrapolated eight characteristics essential for success.

- A bias for action.
- Close to the customer.
- Autonomy.
- Productivity through people.
- Hands-on, value-driven management.
- Sticking to the knitting.
- Simple forms, lean staff.
- Simultaneous loose-tight properties.

In a subsequent work with Austin, *A Passion for Excellence*, Peters reduces the eight points to three fundamental factors: care of customers, innovation and concern for people linked by what Peters calls 'management by walking about' (MBWA), i.e. proactive leadership.

The work of Peters and Waterman inspired parallel studies in a number of Western countries; in Britain Goldsmith and Clutterbuck published *The Winning Streak* in 1984. Their study paralleled *In Search of Excellence* in a number of important respects.

- Visible top management with clear objectives.
- Autonomy for natural work units.
- Balancing tight controls with areas of flexibility.
- High levels of commitment and involvement.
- Emphasis on customer satisfaction.
- Sticking to the basic principles of the business.
- Commitment to innovation and change.
- Integrity in all dealings.

There were substantial criticisms of the 'excellence approach'. A number of the companies cited ran into severe difficulties almost immediately following publication and the research methodology was criticised as superficial and anecdotal. However, the impact of the movement cannot be denied if only for changing the language of management.

Peters has recognised the problems and the changing environment in his work, *Thriving on Chaos* (1988). Rather than trying to establish immutable principles, Peters now argues for organisational uniqueness with highly responsive management style and structure based on:

- obsessional responsiveness to customers;
- constant innovation;
- empowering individuals;
- leadership based on an inspiring vision;
- the introduction of simple quantifiable control systems.

The parallels with the precepts of the TQM gurus are clear and serve to reinforce the view that there may be a minimalist view of the principles informing quality management.

Kanter

Rosabeth Moss Kanter is regarded as one of the most intellectually and academically robust of the writers on excellence. Her books *The Change Masters*

(1983) and *When Giants Learn to Dance* (1989) provide a sophisticated analysis of the social and organisational issues influencing corporate success or failure. As with Peters her preoccupation is with change and it is almost possible to reduce her writing to a simple hypothesis:

Excellence = The Capacity to Change.

She argues that a change culture has the following characteristics:

- It encourages people to be enterprising, to solve problems by operating organisational systems, practices and rewards that reinforce and encourage innovative behaviour.
- It is based on small teams that have autonomy and are able to complete a specified task.
- It has a 'culture of pride' which respects individual creativity and problem-solving ability and denies mediocrity and inferiority.

Her more detailed prescriptions (again the almost mystical points) include references to participation, choice, openness, commitment, explicit standards, rewarding success and creating excitement.

Quality in school management

The purpose of this section is to integrate what has been examined so far in this chapter and to propose a model for total quality management in schools. It is not intended to propose a blueprint, since, as has already been stressed, each organisation must develop its own approach. What follows is a series of proposals to help in the analysis of existing management strategies and to serve as the basis for the formulation of a strategy. This chapter has very briefly highlighted the components of the major theories and illustrations of total quality in practice – obviously not all of what has been described is relevant to schools.

Figure 2.3 is a representation of the components of total quality as they might be applied to schools. The components are derived from the theory and practice described so far in this chapter distilled into the four key components of principles, people, prevention and processes.

Principles The core purpose, vision and values of the school expressed through its leadership and articulated in its mission statement.

People The school is designed around people; it is flat, uses a team-based approach, places enormous emphasis on learning and development and stresses the importance of human relationships.

Prevention The school works to minimise if not eliminate failure; prevention is a shared philosophy applied to all activities.

Processes Every organisational process is seen in terms of the extent to which it meets customer needs.

The vital thing about these components of total quality in schools is that, as shown in Figure 2.3, the four elements are interdependent. Indeed, what is distinctive about total quality is the emphasis on the total: each of the four components contributes to the other to create an holistic view of management. Each of these elements is explored in detail in subsequent chapters. Most schools will have substantial components in place – the quality school has them all to some degree and is actively committed to improving in each respect.

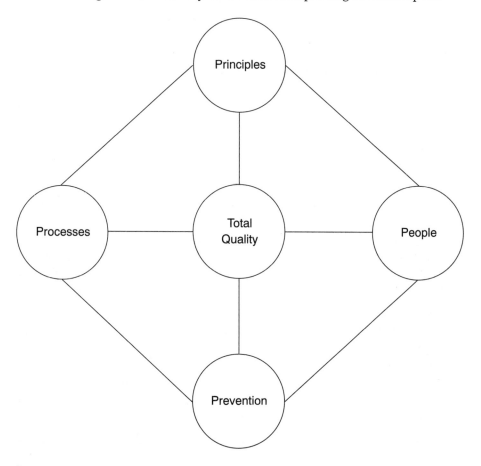

Figure 2.3 The components of total quality

The following review may help to analyse the extent to which your school is on the way to total quality.

Total quality in schools – diagnostic review

Review the extent to which your school meets the criteria for total quality.

Principles

1. The core purpose of the school is explicit.

Not at all   Totally

  1   2   3   4   5

2. The school's vision is known, shared and understood.

Not at all   Totally

  1   2   3   4   5

3. The school's mission permeates all management processes.

Not at all   Totally

  1   2   3   4   5

4. Consistent values inform decision-making.

Not at all   Totally

  1   2   3   4   5

5. Leadership and management are differentiated.

Not at all   Totally

  1   2   3   4   5

6. Leadership is widely distributed.

Not at all   Totally

  1   2   3   4   5

7. Planning is central to management processes.

Not at all   Totally

  1   2   3   4   5

People

8. School structure and processes are team based.

Not at all   Totally

  1   2   3   4   5

9. There is a strong emphasis on effective personal relationships.

Not at all   Totally

  1   2   3   4   5

10. Authority and responsibility are devolved.

Not at all   Totally

  1   2   3   4   5

11. There is equity in terms of social facilities.

Not at all   Totally

  1   2   3   4   5

12. Individuals have significant control over their own development.

Not at all   Totally

  1   2   3   4   5

13. Development of others is a high priority for all managers.

Not at all   Totally

  1   2   3   4   5

14. Decision-making is fully participative.

Not at all   Totally

  1   2   3   4   5

Prevention

15. Processes are managed to prevent failure.

Not at all   Totally

  1   2   3   4   5

16. All key processes are defined and specified.

Not at all   Totally

  1   2   3   4   5

17. Measurement is used to improve processes.

Not at all   Totally

  1   2   3   4   5

18. Management works to achieve consistency and eliminate variation.

Not at all   Totally

  1   2   3   4   5

19. Monitoring and evaluation are built into every process.

Not at all   Totally

  1   2   3   4   5

20. Documentation is produced to consistent standards.

Not at all   Totally

  1   2   3   4   5

21. Appropriate external validation of quality assurance strategies is sought.

Not at all   Totally

  1   2   3   4   5

Customers

22. Each process is designed on the basis of the needs of the individual customer.

Not at all				Totally
1	2	3	4	5

23. The school is organised around the needs of individual learners.

Not at all				Totally
1	2	3	4	5

24. There is a public commitment continuously to improve the services provided to customers.

Not at all				Totally
1	2	3	4	5

25. Customer satisfaction is regularly surveyed and acted on.

Not at all				Totally
1	2	3	4	5

26. The needs of internal and external customers are recognised.

Not at all				Totally
1	2	3	4	5

27. Customers are fully integrated into the design and delivery of services.

Not at all				Totally
1	2	3	4	5

28. For us 'Quality is what the customer says it is'.

Not at all				Totally
1	2	3	4	5

Total your scores for each section:

Principles	People	Prevention	Customers
1	8	15	22
2	9	16	23
3	10	17	24
4	11	18	25
5	12	19	26
6	13	20	27
7	14	21	28
———	———	———	———

What are the implications of your scores?

Another way to understand total quality is to identify a number of key precepts which capture the essence of the distinctive nature of the approach. These have been described as the 'clichés of quality' and their frequent use can diminish their impact. However, they can help to create the new organisational vocabulary that the implementation of total quality requires.

1 **Focus on the customer:** this is axiomatic to total quality. The customer is the *raison d'être* of the organisation and also provides the definition of quality.

2 **Fitness for purpose:** quality is defined by the extent to which a product or service is fit or appropriate for the purposes as defined by the customer, not the supplier.

3 **Prevention not inspection:** in order to guarantee fitness for purpose the emphasis has to be on preventing failure not in finding out that something has gone wrong after the event and then having to put things right. (Right First Time and zero defects are related concepts.)

4 **Understanding the cost of non-conformance:** this relates to the significance of measurement and the use of techniques to establish, during the process, the extent to which the requirements of a specification are being adhered to.

5 **Continuous improvement:** this is a core concept and one of the defining characteristics of total quality. It describes the commitment to seeking ways of improving the service to customers and of enhancing the effectiveness of the organisation itself.

6 **Drive out fear:** the only way to a climate of improvement is to create a culture which is based on positive regard and a sense of being able to learn.

7 **Moments of truth:** this refers to the importance of customer perceptions as the basis for all decisions. Moments of truth are those incidents when the customer actually experiences the product or service and the extent to which the organisation has kept its promise is determined. Our lives are made up of hundreds of moments of truth – all of them significant.

Summary

- Total quality is increasingly the norm in industrial and commercial organisations.
- Total quality is a specific term that has to be distinguished from quality control and quality assurance.
- There is a voluminous literature on quality and excellence but the key issues can be distilled into a few precepts.
- Adopting TQ is an explanation of the dominance of a number of well known organisations.
- It is possible to isolate a number of features of TQ theory that are not specific to the commercial sector.

Action

1   If you use the word quality in your school's aims what exactly do you mean by it?

2   Have you identified your school's clients? Is your view shared by all your colleagues?

3   Is your senior management team really a team or just a meeting?

4   Does your school prepare its pupils for work in a TQ company?

5   How well do you communicate as a manager? How do you know?

6   If you reject the experience of industry and commerce do you have an equally systematic alternative?

7   If schools are not about managing quality then what are they about?

3

■ ■ ■

Customers

Introduction

The quality organisation exists for its customers and has no purpose other than providing products and services that satisfy customer needs. The commercial organisation which fails to meet its customers' requirements will rapidly go out of business. The rest of this book is devoted to principles and processes to help ensure a focus on the customer. This chapter is concerned with explaining the issues involved in the concept of 'the customer'. There are many problems associated with using the term customer in an education context; there is no cash transaction, education is a statutory requirement, in many parts of the country there is no choice of school so the notion of customer choice is spurious. More significant are the objections that education involves professional relationships so the term 'client' is more appropriate, and that the role of schools is not to perpetuate existing social norms but rather to enhance society, to pass on moral, intellectual and social skills to children.

This view presupposes a unique body of knowledge to which access is restricted – teachers are the custodians of that knowledge and transmit it according to best professional practice. The customer can't know best because the customer doesn't know. A quality approach denies the validity of this view and the 1988 Education Reform Act has done much to challenge it by giving parents the potential power to choose. Many trends in schools have highlighted the issue of responsiveness to children, community and the full range of stakeholders in education.

The purpose of this chapter is to examine the components of customer satisfaction through a variety of issues:

- defining the customer;
- the nature of quality customer service;
- ensuring customer satisfaction.

Defining the customer

In Figure 3.1 two types of supplier–customer relationship are shown. Figure 3.1(A) caricatures the traditional customer relationship in education – passive recipients being talked about rather than listened to – a relationship that is easy to parody – 'no parents past this point'; 'generally satisfactory work and progress'; the options booklet that assumes training in deductive logic; the school prospectus written by teachers for teachers; the exclusion of non-teachers from the staffroom; homework instructions so cryptic that the time allocated is spent deciphering them. These are all minor irritants and are symptomatic of a failure to perceive customer needs and expectations.

The academic debate about who is the customer in education is capable of metaphysical convolutions; working on permutations of professionality,

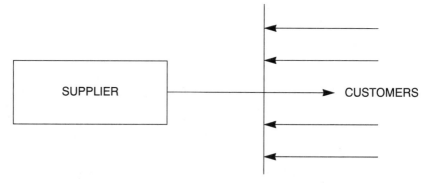

(A)   Traditional supplier – customer relationship

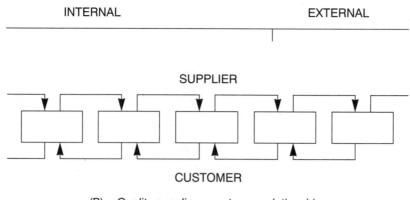

(B)   Quality supplier – customer relationships

Figure 3.1 Supplier–customer relationships

professionalism, accountability and answerability a wide range of answers is possible. The total quality response is quite simple and is central to this book.

> A CUSTOMER IS ANYONE TO WHOM
>
> A PRODUCT OR SERVICE IS PROVIDED

A customer is therefore defined in terms of relationships and processes rather than relative status, role or function. Customers can be both internal and external and the quality approach to them is shown in Figure 3.1(B).

The implications of this model are:

- Everyone is a supplier and a customer.
- There are equal responsibilities on suppliers and customers.
- Work processes have to be defined in terms of customers and suppliers.
- It may be helpful to differentiate between internal and external customers and suppliers but not to discriminate in levels of service.
- Supplier–customer 'chains' may be of variable length but this cannot be used as an excuse to compromise the process.

In order to ensure the integrity of the chain a significant amount of analysis is required to establish who exactly is involved; unless this first step is taken quality will be problematic.

Figure 3.2 shows the supplier–customer relationship involved in organising a class trip to a museum. Unless all the participants are identified it will be impossible to identify all requirements and so impossible to provide quality service.

If one component is missing then the information flow will be incomplete and the trip will probably not take place. There may be associated processes, e.g. the teacher liaising with the headteacher, with the bus company etc. Each link in the chain has to be of equal strength; the information from the museum has to be complete – opening times, eating facilities, educational support services, prices etc. However, this will be to no avail if the letter is not typed and copied in time, if children do not deliver it and if parents do not have a date by which to return it. At each stage requirements have to be stated so that customers and suppliers are aware of their interdependence.

In this example parents might be regarded as the 'final' customer and their needs therefore determine the whole process. In order to make the process a quality one the needs of the final customer have to be clearly understood and

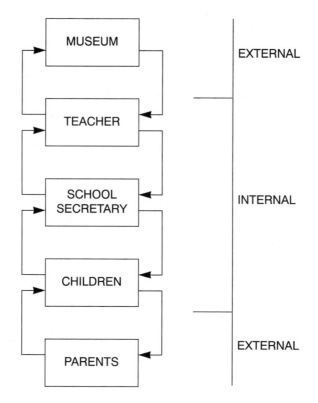

Figure 3.2 Supplier–customer relationships in organising a school trip

expressed in such a way as to inform the design and delivery of the process. This involves defining the customer and then developing mechanisms to ensure monitoring and feedback. These mechanisms are discussed in the third section of this chapter, 'Ensuring customer satisfaction'; defining the customer involves understanding a complex range of factors, as shown in Figure 3.3.

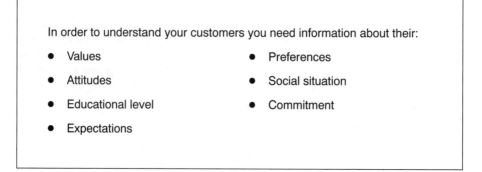

Figure 3.3 Defining the customer

Many schools could argue that they have a full understanding of their customers. However, care has to be taken in the extent to which this understanding is imposed by teachers, is based on subjective opinion or is swayed by political opinion.

The components of defining the customer outlined in Figure 3.3 may be expanded.

Values

This is the significance attached to the educational process in general and the school in particular. It will be reflected in the extent to which education is seen by parents as an investment or an expedient, the importance attached to the school by the community and the credibility it has with other stakeholders. Unless the school understands the values of its customers it is unlikely to be able to deliver quality outcomes.

Attitudes

In some senses attitudes might be regarded as the manifestation of values – responses to the school, displayed in behaviour. Attitudes are reflected in the language, involvement and commitment of the school's customers. The school that aspires to provide a quality service to its customers looks to itself first as the cause of behaviour on the part of its clients. Attitudes change and develop in response to the service provided.

Educational level

Most professionals are so immersed in their expertise that it is possible to forget that the rest of the community does not necessarily share their understanding. Just as teachers are sometimes confused by medical or legal language so their clients can be intimidated by inappropriate language.

No effective teacher would ever dream of teaching a lesson without checking that the vocabulary was appropriate and the concepts understood. The same principle applies to all those with whom the school communicates. This is not to argue for simplification to the point of absurdity but rather that any communication be effective.

Expectations

Meeting customer expectations is the hallmark of quality – exceeding them is the key characteristic of total quality. However, this means that they have to be known and understood. Expectations are more than requirements – they are the basis of 'delighting the customer'. It is easy for a garage or shop to exceed customer expectations, less so for a school to ensure that every child is happy and fulfilled, achieves at least five GCSE passes or gets a job. Yet one of the principal features of successful schools is that they share and express high expectations.

Preferences

All organisations that provide a service will usually offer a range of options in order to maximise the possibilities of anticipating customer choice. Understanding the broad preferences of customers is a fundamental component of providing a quality service. The details are to be negotiated and developed on the basis of feedback but the broad pattern of preferences has to be established; this might include issues such as uniform, the pattern of the school day, sex education, religious education etc.

Social situation

The social context of a school will be a major determinant of its response to many of its customers. Prevailing patterns of culture, the ethnic balance, unemployment, the economic situation, social advantage and deprivation will all be significant features in helping to determine a school's response to its community.

Schools are often highly expert in understanding the context in which they operate. The difference for a TQM school is the extent to which responses are assumed and derived by teachers or based on real understanding.

Commitment

Commercial success depends on obtaining and retaining customers. Increasingly schools are in the same situation – failure to recruit and retain pupils will result in the school ceasing to be viable. It is therefore essential to understand the significance attached to education by customers, in order to be able to make the most appropriate responses. Figure 3.4 shows one way of understanding the implications of varying levels of commitment.

For a relatively prosperous community the relative levels of significance might appear as shown in the figure; however, the situation could be totally reversed in other communities. The commitment of parents will be a direct function of the significance attached to education and this will in turn reflect the six components identified earlier.

Defining the customer is essential with regard to parents and children and they should be the predominant feature of any such analysis. However, the same

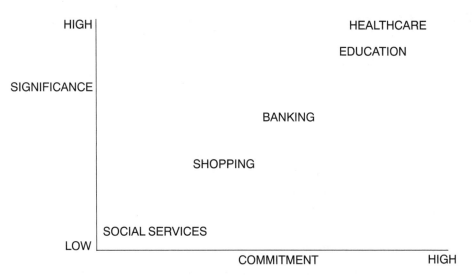

Figure 3.4 Understanding the relationship between significance and commitment

process is needed for all customers, especially external ones. There is a potential issue in that perceptions and needs may be in conflict – different groups may have varying expectations. This issue is best resolved by analysis of the particular process and identifying the 'end user' who is then the customer whose needs predominate. This does not mean that managing a quality school is simply a series of conditioned responses. There is an imperative to enhance the service provided, to 'delight the customer' and most importantly to add value. Total quality organisations are successful because they build on customer expectations and continually enhance the service provided. But the starting-point must be the values, attitudes, educational level, expectations, preferences, social situations and commitment of customers.

One of the most significant concerns to emerge about the focus on the customer in education is the issue of whether the customer is always right. This can best be expressed through the tension between needs and wants. A professional perspective on needs may not coincide with a pupil's view of wants. Two quality concepts are relevant here.

First, it is incumbent on suppliers to 'delight their customers', i.e. to inform and educate so that they understand the nature of the service being offered. Needs can become wants if the customer is made aware and helped to understand.

Second, the customer is not always right. Demanding an epicurean meal at a motorway service area is inappropriate and cannot be provided. However, it is appropriate in a restaurant with a Michelin star. The supplier has to state what is being offered and then ensure that it is supplied according to the agreed specification.

The nature of quality customer service

This is the aspect of quality management most easy to misunderstand and misapply. Customer service is not about potted plants, carpets, glossy brochures and carefully scripted receptionists. These factors can be significant but are only manifestations of a fundamental obsession with satisfying the customer. There is a temptation to assume that smartness equals quality but there is little point if the appropriate person is not available and if the quality of children's learning is not the central focus of any discussion. Reviews of the literature on customer service produce lists of strategies, many of which fall into the 'have a nice day' syndrome. However, it is possible to isolate a range of factors which are appropriate to schools.

Conformance to requirements

This is at the heart of quality management. In essence it means that the service provided is fit for the purpose intended, i.e. it meets the needs of the customer. There are many potential applications of this principle in schools:

- reporting on progress to parents: the information is expressed in such a way as to be comprehensible and comprehensive;
- purchase of text books: they are relevant, up to date, written at an appropriate level with a suitable format;
- classroom organisation: facilities and resources are easily available.

This list could be continued indefinitely and it is an important part of the implementation process to discover and fulfil these needs. However, the most important potential application is in the organisation of learning. Conformance to requirements does raise significant questions about the delivery of the curriculum. If the needs of the individual learner are considered the starting point for identifying customer needs then a number of issues emerge:

- the need to relate learning strategies to individual ability;
- the flexible use of time to allow appropriate pacing and completion of integrated units of study;
- deployment of the full range of teaching strategies from the most didactic to the most flexible, to be determined by need not ideology;
- reviewing the role of the teacher as controller and emphasising the role of facilitator;
- questioning teaching the 'class' when individual outcomes are the determinants of educational success;
- recognition of the importance of intellectual and social skills development being reflected in the organisation of learning;
- ensuring that marking and assessment are formative rather than summative;

- programming options to ensure that individual rather than systems needs are met.

This approach would appear to endorse an open or flexible learning approach and be the strategy closest to quality principles. However, a quality approach to managing learning is not a matter of prescribing the 'one best way' but rather of diagnosing and identifying needs and relating learning strategies to them. What the quality approach does question is the view of managing learning for administrative convenience. As has been mentioned elsewhere in this book the effective primary classroom is probably the closest that education currently comes to total quality.

An outstanding example of creating learning resources that are fit for purpose is provided by Hannon (1996) in her description of a project to help student teachers respond appropriately to pupils with special educational needs, especially those in hospital. A science project, focusing on the five senses, resulted in the production of boxes 'filled with activities, models, teaching materials, work cards for children and notes for the teacher' (p. 117). Fitness for purpose was achieved through the development of criteria. There should be:

- evidence that the work in the box is related to the National Curriculum Science;
- a high standard of presentation of materials;
- guidance for both pupil and teacher;
- a variety of recording ideas for children within their various limitations;
- potential for extension of Science;
- potential for cross-curricular work;
- an opportunity to empathise with the special needs associated with the impairment of one sense.

In this example purpose is clearly indicated as learning in the context of National Curriculum Science, fitness is defined by the specific needs of the pupils:

> *Activities in the boxes were bright and attractive to sick children and incorporated a range of Science activities and recording methods accessible to children with different types of disability. Some of the teaching materials were made waterproof for hygienic reasons. Others gave children, who could not write easily, an opportunity to place their responses by adhering labels or pictures by velcro.* (ibid.)

In each respect the learning materials conform to the requirements of a range of criteria which recognised both the educational needs and the specific needs of the individual learner.

Continuous improvement

In terms of customer satisfaction continuous improvement means that suppliers are constantly concerned with adding value. There is an obsession with enhancing and improving every process. This is where professional expertise and development are so important. It is the professional skills and knowledge of teachers and managers in schools that are the principle source of this process. At the most fundamental level it is how the teaching of a particular topic can be improved the next time it is taught and how teaching aids and resources can be deployed to better effect.

The concept of continuous improvement is powerfully captured by Collarbone (1997) who relates the story of improvement at Haggerston School as a journey, the perfect metaphor for continuous improvement:

As we journey forward we are now aware of all the signposts that we ignore at our peril:

- Develop a common vocabulary that encapsulates the vision – a common language that all can understand.

- Set the exit points high.

- Believe fundamentally that you can meet the exit points and make sure that all your limitations are focused on that end point.

- Look for examples of good practice and make sure that everyone knows about them.

- Talk up the school, the pupils, the parents and the staff at every opportunity and make sure they hear it.

- Review, review, review at every stage and act on the information you receive.

- Above all, be confident, be bold, be determined. (p. 29)

This is a natural process for professionals – never accepting the status quo but constantly explaining techniques to ensure a more complete understanding, to improve the language used in materials, to develop activities that help clarify complex issues.

The same principles apply to management processes in schools: induction procedures, decision-making, INSET days are all capable of sustaining improvement over time. The crucial thing is that there is no complacency, no notion of a plateau of acceptability.

Responsiveness

This is one of the most tangible expressions of a customer satisfaction orientation. In practical terms it means rapid response to complaints and requests: the phone is answered promptly, letters are replied to within a specified time period, and more importantly, there is a tangible and personal response on the customers' terms. This might mean an 'open door' policy. It certainly means concerns are given a high degree of seriousness.

In the classroom it means creating the situation where children feel able, and are encouraged, to express concerns which are dealt with. It also means that ideas and suggestions are incorporated rapidly in order to improve classroom and school processes.

Integration

Customers are fully integrated into the organisation. This means that possible customer response is the baseline criterion in every decision-making process and that customers are physically incorporated into activities. It is better to involve at the outset than to decide, consult and then change. An example of a high level of integration is found in the National Commission (1996) report on Crowcroft Primary School. The key features underpinning parental involvement are:

- the high level of respect for and the valuing of parents;
- the high level of information exchange and genuine consultation;
- shared decision-making; support and training of parents;
- access for all parents and care givers regardless of personal circumstances, culture or language. (p. 62)

This is much more than encouraging a PTA, holding parents' evenings or inviting parents to help. It is actively, deliberately and systematically informing and involving all customers in processes. Low levels of interest are usually explained by low levels of perceived significance. Genuine integration means that customers will be able to see tangible outcomes of their involvement rather than a token acknowledgement.

In practical terms this means maximum contact at appropriate levels: in the secondary school making the form tutor the first point of contact with parents; the notion of the 'open day' being replaced by the concept of permanent openness. The non-teaching staff of the school need to be fully incorporated into all aspects of the quality strategy. Crucially, administrative systems and structures should not be used as barriers to incorporation and involvement. Secondary and primary school staff need to visit and exchange as do secondary and college staff. The National Curriculum requires partnership through integration if it is to work for the benefit of children. Many schools have found that the best way to deal with bullying, theft, vandalism etc. is not to make more rules but to hand the problem, its solution and implementation to the children themselves.

This is a classic example of real integration and it is much more likely to succeed because it takes into account the views of those involved, and it also has their commitment. This is listening to the customer and demonstrating tangible respect.

Focus on delivery

The quality organisation centres all its resources on those in direct contact with the customer. In the case of schools this is obviously the classroom teacher. The focus for concern, support and development has to be those who actually deliver. Their development must be the central priority and the way in which the school is managed should reflect the importance of the classroom teacher. They are the management team's most important internal customer: the best word to describe the relationship between management team and teacher is probably respect, i.e. recognition of the central significance of the classroom practitioner.

One of the best ways of achieving customer satisfaction is to ensure that those with whom customers come into contact have the skills to be able to respond to and confide in senior management. This requires support, praise, recognition, thanks and trust. In practical terms it means direct and immediate support for teachers in the classroom, budgeting so as to maximise resources at the focal point of the school and the provision of quality INSET to meet classroom needs.

A further manifestation of this is the involvement of senior management by being directly available to classroom teachers and by being involved in the classroom and other aspects of the school on a regular basis. This can take a wide variety of forms, e.g. covering for absence, having a programme of regular cover to create opportunities for feedback, and to create time for colleagues by taking teachers off timetables for a week to allow for projects etc.

The crucial thing is that managers do not 'lose touch' and are directly available to improve responsiveness. Much is made in the literature of the quality movement of 'management by walking about' (MBWA). Better than this is LBDTJ – leading by doing the job. This is not to diminish the strategic role of senior management, but rather to stress the importance of keeping close to the customer and seeing the school through its customers' eyes.

Practical ways of keeping a 'focus on delivery', i.e. emphasising the centrality of pupil learning, include:

- putting learning on the agenda of every meeting;
- setting up coaching, peer support, teaching partnerships in order to explore learning and teaching strategies;
- making learning significant by its being the central theme of the majority of INSET sessions;
- encouraging all staff and students to keep learning journals – to reflect on what has been learned and, more importantly, how it was learned;
- building in review to every process – at the end of every lesson, day, project or meeting a quick and simple review can be carried out;
- publicly celebrating examples of success to help create a shared understanding and to reinforce the core purpose of the school.

Listening to the customer

An insight into how listening to customers is possible right the way through the education service is provided by Carol Jefferson (1994), headteacher of Humberstone Junior School, Leicester.

The opportunity to try something out came when a colleague's arrival was delayed one morning. I asked her class: 'If I had a magic wand and could magic anything into school that you wanted and could magic out anything you didn't like, what would you like me to do?'

I took some notes and asked the children how I could get information from other children in the school. They suggested that I ask them the same question and ask for writing or pictures (or both) so that everyone could have a chance to respond.

One hundred and eighty children (out of three hundred and seven) replied to me, across the whole age range (7–11). As one would expect, behaviour moderation was high on their list of urgent concerns. More than 50% of the responses demanded that a stop should be put to bullying, but also, that there should be no fighting, stealing, kicking, blackmail, name calling and racism. On the more positive side, children wanted to see more kindness, sharing and friendly people. Other comments tended to highlight episodes of bad behaviour that had affected us all recently – and they told me that they wanted to see an end to swearing, talking in quiet time, shouting, being cheeky, spitting and flooding the toilets. It did rather paint a very gloomy picture of the perception of behaviour in my school.

The result of this particular section of the survey is that there has been a complete review of our school rules and for the first time in our school, a formal policy on encouraging good behaviour has been drafted, including the children's own ideas about which sanctions should be employed. These include writing letters of apology in their own time and, in extreme circumstances, children being banned from school at lunchtime.

Quality customer service can only be achieved through real listening; this topic is the subject of the third section of this chapter. Delivering quality customer service is a matter of acknowledging the uniqueness of each customer, treating them with respect and listening to them.

Ensuring customer satisfaction

Measuring customer satisfaction is at the heart of total quality – obtaining feedback and acting on it is what differentiates total quality from every other management theory. There is a moral obligation on all suppliers to find out customer needs, to seek to meet them and then to find out the extent to which they have been met. There is an equal obligation on customers to articulate requirements and then to participate in monitoring and review. This section is concerned with some of the methods available to gather data. Many of these will be familiar to most schools, but the crucial difference is the extent to which listening takes place and action results.

Techniques appropriate for schools

Suggestion cards

Invite all the school's customers, internal and external, to suggest improvements. The natural creativity of children can be a powerful force, as can parents themselves after spending two hours in school for only twenty minutes' consultation with teachers. The rule is to offer solutions to the problems as well as identifying them. This approach can also be used to solve a particular problem. The important thing is that the cards are seen to lead to action and are not used as a spurious form of PR.

Shadowing

Suppliers place themselves in the situation of customers: a form teacher in a secondary school spends the whole day with her form (and is not allowed in the staffroom at break or lunchtime); a primary teacher joins his former pupils on their first day in secondary school; a secondary timetabler tastes the fruits of her labours by experiencing the reality of the pro-graph board; senior staff teach the problem class.

Although the shadow's presence will inevitably distort 'reality' the process does provide the opportunity for experiencing the direct impact of school policies.

Interviews

These can be used with almost any group as the basis for detailed and informed data collection. Talking to small groups of children, inviting representatives of the local community, groups of governors and teachers to indicate how the school might be improved are all potentially powerful strategies to generate ideas, to indicate seriousness and demonstrate commitment.

Surveys

These are probably the most powerful, and potentially most intimidating means of obtaining feedback. They are important because they are capable of quantification and will thus permit comparisons over time. Quantification also facilitates prioritisation. Surveys can be used to:

- collect information about customer needs;
- identify specific problems;
- assess conformity to requirements;
- measure satisfaction.

Thus surveys may be used about a specific lesson, a particular aspect of school life, meetings, evaluation of a course of study, a specific facility (e.g. the library) or views on a current issue (e.g. uniform).

The design of the survey should be determined by the data required but may include:

- open-ended questions – a useful source of data but difficult to analyse;
- closed questions – easy to analyse but limited options;
- rating scales – easy to complete and analyse but requiring careful design.

The data collected can be analysed using a variety of techniques such as Pareto analysis. The results of a survey can provide:

- instant feedback;
- diagnosis of specific problem areas;
- indications of satisfaction and success;
- decisions about priorities for action;
- evidence of commitment to customer satisfaction.

Team meetings

Almost any team can contribute feedback by having a regular agenda item concerned with feedback to suppliers. It may be appropriate to constitute teams for the specific purpose of reviewing services provided. A team may also invite some of its customers to attend meetings on a regular basis. Aspects of some lessons, e.g. personal and social education, can be devoted to the provision of feedback. This survey is potentially one of the most powerful as it integrates review and feedback into normal operating processes. As confidence grows within a team so feedback will become more detailed and specific.

Although review and monitoring are essential they are symptomatic of a school which is listening to its customers and trying to see itself through their eyes. If the customer chain is fully established then there will be a gradual shift from reaction to anticipation and the school's customers will be fully integrated into all aspects of its working processes. The full involvement of children in this process can be viewed as an important, and living contribution to their preparation for adulthood by learning how to participate in a wide range of social processes – not least their own obligations as suppliers of products and services. Seeing children as customers in the classroom and school processes also minimises the view that management approaches turn them into products.

Summary

- Quality organisations exist to meet customer needs.
- A customer is anyone to whom a product or service is provided.
- There are internal and external customers.
- It is the responsibility of customers to specify needs, and of suppliers to meet them.
- Customers need to be defined in terms of a complex range of factors.
- Customer needs are defined in specific actions.
- Customers must be listened to – complaints and concerns must be welcomed.
- A range of techniques can be used to find out about customer satisfaction.
- Children are not products – they are customers.

Action

1   Identify your customers and find out their requirements.
2   Analyse areas of strength and weakness.
3   Build review procedures into every process.
4   Create a climate for delighting the customer.

4
■ ■ ■

Quality Assurance

Introduction

Quality organisations are obsessed with measurement. Every aspect of every process is measured and one of the first signs of trusting the work force is delegation of responsibility for statistical processes to operative level. Measurement is used to ensure conformity to standards, to identify the cost of deviation and to monitor the impact of improvements. Very limited changes in vocabulary are necessary to find parallels in schools – the use of registers, marking and assessment, reading ages and setting are all forms of quantification used in the management of children's learning. This chapter argues that a similar approach is necessary in the management of all school processes. Four main issues are discussed:

- understanding processes in schools;
- the cost of quality;
- understanding variation and prevention;
- quality standards.

The key purpose of improving work processes is to add value, to make the process and thereby its product closer to customer requirements and so of higher quality. Adding value is a matter of listening to customers and making modifications in the light of their feedback. Each improvement, each development makes it more likely that the product or process will conform to expectations of customers and so retain their loyalty. Adding value is not a matter of embellishment or increasing complexity but getting ever closer to customer specification. In schools, for example, this does not necessarily mean more resources; it means meetings that solve problems, lessons that are understood, INSET days that can be applied in practical terms.

Understanding processes in schools

Education processes are extraordinarily complex given the enormous variability of inputs, the interactions that take place and the often ambiguous outcomes. If education is perceived as a lifelong process with most of the factors outside the control of schools then it could be argued that it is impossible to analyse the process. However, this is to deny or minimise the reality of school life which is made up of concrete activities most of which are planned and structured and for which the inputs are carefully calculated and deployed. Although classroom processes are complex, and properly the subject of another book, management processes in schools are appropriate for analysis. The objective of all management processes is to meet the requirements of the customer; 'problems' in the management of schools are almost invariably due to a failure in a process which can be analysed and corrected. In its simplest form, a work process has the components shown in Figure 4.1.

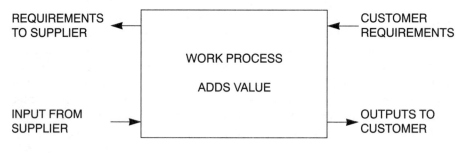

Figure 4.1 Work processes

The work process can be seen as a link in the customer–supplier chain and it requires:

- articulation and communication of customer requirements;
- articulation and communication of requirements of the supplier;
- the provision of the skills, resources and procedures necessary to complete the process.

If this third element is added then the process model becomes much more detailed, as shown in Figure 4.2.

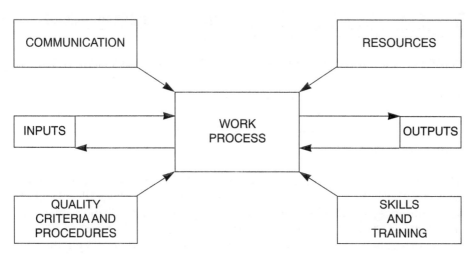

Figure 4.2 The components of work processes

In order for the process to work all the aspects identified have to be complete; lack of definition in any respect will compromise the potential to meet the customer requirements: a simple example – a letter to parents about a trip – illustrates the point.

The supplier is the teacher planning the trip. The requirements on her are to supply the school secretary with all the necessary data presented in a legible form.

The customer is a parent whose requirements include:

- all the relevant data expressed in a clear format;
- plenty of time;
- a clear indication of what action is required.

The process is managed by the secretary who needs time to complete the task, access to the word processor and photocopier, school guidelines on the format of the letter, procedures for distribution, the time to check the letter with the teacher. This all assumes skills with the word processor and photocopier – not to be taken for granted.

All of these elements are necessary if there is to be a quality product. This example may be trivial but the implications of not managing the process are substantial.

- Time is wasted by teacher and secretary in checking, clarifying or correcting.
- Reworking the letter would double the cost in terms of time, paper and copying.
- If the letter is sent out incomplete then time would be wasted in answering queries.
- Incorrect information might result in a limited response so causing the trip to be cancelled.

The financial cost of reissuing such a letter might be £50 (£12 for teacher time, £8 secretarial time, £5 copying x 2) and this is avoidable waste. Few teachers would throw away £25 worth of stock but many will lose much more in wasted time because of a failure to prevent errors. This direct waste is matched, at least, by the frustration, loss of credibility, opportunity cost and poor reputation for efficiency arising from such an incident.

It is comparatively easy to assign a cash value to a range of examples: a senior management team meeting that fails to reach a solution to a problem and has to reconvene could be costed at £100; the social cost is significantly higher. A primary school staff meeting where a circular is read to the staff for thirty minutes probably costs £40 in terms of salary but far more in resentment and a sense of powerlessness.

To ensure the optimum use of resources the emphasis in managing has to be on prevention – one of the cornerstones of total quality. In the example just described the costs resulting from an incorrect letter were discovered by inspection, i.e. after the event, and therefore had to be corrected; the additional costs arose from inspection itself and could have been negated by a policy of prevention, i.e. finding out needs and working to established procedures: prevention must be built into working procedures.

Prevention in an industrial context is very much concerned with establishing a range of highly detailed statistical process control techniques. It is difficult, if not impossible to translate these into an educational environment. However, there is a model in the use of testing in the classroom – if that test is used to modify teaching strategies rather than simply recorded, and used as a measure of ignorance rather than feedback on teaching methods. Some possible applications of these techniques to management processes are outlined in Chapter 10.

Prevention is directly linked to knowledge; it is a central responsibility of management to ensure that requirements and standards are public, explicit and understood. Failure to articulate requirements makes conformity impossible. It is therefore necessary to implement a range of strategies which make quality intrinsic to every operation.

Quality policy

This is driven by the school's mission; it is a declaration of hope, aspiration and ambition and it spells out what quality means. The components of a quality policy might include:

- a definition of quality for the school;
- the systems to be applied to obtain that quality;
- customer orientation;
- respect for the individual;
- the significance of training and development;
- management commitment;
- responsibility for quality.

Operating procedures

Many of the problems that occur in schools are due to a breakdown in working procedures. This is the fault of managers whose responsibility it is to ensure that operating procedures are clear, understood and capable of implementation. The failure of a process says more about the system and its designer than it does about the people who operate it. Schools often have published procedures for basic processes, e.g. marking registers – however, if a process is significant (and if it is not, why continue it?) it requires an operating procedure. The best examples of operating procedures in schools are syllabuses and schemes of work.

Operating procedures are appropriate for:

- marking, recording and assessment;
- managing pastoral care issues;
- relationship with external bodies – police, social services etc.;
- health and safety issues record keeping;
- consultative procedures;
- homework;
- stock control;
- applying for courses;
- disciplinary matters;
- parents' evenings;
- option arrangements;
- handling finances;
- planning trips;
- transfer to secondary school, post-compulsory education.

There is obviously a danger that itemising procedures in detail could become a bureaucratic nightmare and if such documents are simply issued they will probably be ignored. However, if the development of these procedures is managed as a quality process in itself they are likely to pervade all aspects of school life. In order to achieve this, procedures need to be developed and improved by the teams that will implement them and they must be written in response to customer requirements. In some instances there will be legal obligations on teachers but in many cases writing the procedures will be the first step towards customer satisfaction. Developing the procedures is a classic example of delegation and trust in action and those who write them will need training.

Once established the procedures should become an essential component of working life, constantly referred to, used in meetings and as a standard reference point. This means that they should be well produced, meeting teachers' needs in terms of language, design and organisation. They might well take the form of a handbook which includes the mission statement, quality policy and job description of all those employed in the school.

The handbook will thus become an essential component of induction, appraisal and development and will provide support for teachers, managers and governors in a wide range of personnel procedures.

Quality criteria

These may well form part of operating procedures; they are necessary to identify exactly the standard of work required – in essence procedures will identify 'who?' 'what?' and 'when?' and the quality criteria will indicate 'how?'. For example, the National Curriculum will specify the content, sequencing and level of a topic; a school's quality criteria will identify the resources to be used, the strategies to be employed, the subject and methods of assessment. The concern here is with consistency of practice and ensuring that every process is delivered to the optimum quality.

One of the most important applications of quality criteria is in the appraisal and staff development policy of a school. Criteria are essential components of the self-review, classroom and task observation and target setting processes. There are two central issues here: first, the appraisal and development process is designed to recognise and reinforce the successes of the teacher and identify development needs. Those needs must be met in accordance with the mission and development plan of the school which are expressed in the quality criteria. Second, the management of the appraisal and professional development processes must, themselves, be quality processes, i.e. quality can only be achieved by delivering quality. The medium is the message.

The implementation of the School Teacher Appraisal Regulations will necessitate the development of criteria for appraisal; it is suggested that the following areas need to be covered:

- relationships with children;
- lesson planning and preparation;
- organisation of the classroom and resources;
- classroom management;
- assessment and monitoring of pupils' progress;
- subject knowledge;
- pastoral care;
- departmental management;
- leadership.

The detailed components of each of these areas need to take into account DES, LEA and diocesan requirements, the provisions of the Education Acts and the community in which the school works.

Monitoring and review

It is important to distinguish between monitoring and inspection in respect of total quality and inspection in the LEA/school context. A total quality organisation strives to eliminate inspection as manifested in quality control (see Chapter 2). HMI and LEAs have a statutory responsibility to inspect schools. In some senses the notion of external inspection is alien to a quality management approach unless advisers and HMI are seen as clients/customers who have rights and duties which the school has to meet.

Therefore it is not inspection in the sense of post-facto fault finding but rather a process of obtaining feedback and advice from two major customers (DES and LEA) on the extent to which requirements are being met.

Within the school, monitoring and review are implicit to every school process, e.g. appraisal team meetings, budget planning, school development plans etc. The important thing is that the process of monitoring and review should be carried out by those actually responsible for the process and that it should become implicit in the way of working. A number of review techniques is outlined in the third section of this chapter. As far as possible the review processes should be specific and focus on the question: 'To what extent have customer requirements been met?' Monitoring should be a regular component of all processes which in time can contribute to a review, i.e. an overview of how they are contributing to the achievement of the school's mission statement.

The cost of quality

One of the great myths surrounding traditional views of quality is that it costs more. This is understandable if quality is viewed as 'goodness', an intangible which has to be struggled for. If goodness is the top of the mountain then it is obvious that the more energy expended the better the chance of getting to the top. However, an analysis of the map might reveal a better route, planning and preparation will minimise the distance covered, appropriate equipment will ease the journey, a greater distance can be covered with less output of energy. Even with the right equipment a wrong turning means wasted effort, having to retrace the journey and start again. Getting it right first time means the objective is achieved at minimum cost.

It takes time, money, effort, skill and knowledge to produce defective services. No manager or teacher in a school will deliberately waste resources, yet a great deal of time will be spent 'reworking', checking and inspecting, all of which are symptomatic of waste. No amount of additional expenditure will improve a faulty system or process; the process itself has to be modified in response to client needs. Figure 4.3 provides a basis for analysing the extent to which non-conformance to customer specifications is responsible for wasted resources of time, skills etc. Every positive response indicates waste. The greater the total the higher the waste and the lower the level of customer satisfaction.

It is not appropriate to blame the people involved: the chances are that they did not conform to requirements because the process was not understood, was inappropriate or badly designed in the first place. The best way to overcome this problem is to redesign the process to ensure that it is driven by customer requirements. This will in turn ensure a higher probability of conformity and thus the delivery of quality.

The traditional approach is demonstrated in Figure 4.4(A): quality is perceived as costing more in proportion to the fewer defects. There is therefore an optimum point after which improving quality means increased costs to customers and thus reduced demand. This approach is symptomatic of many Western companies and explains their decline relative to their Japanese competitors. It might also help to indicate why two schools with the same budget, serving similar communities achieve remarkably different outcomes. In essence it is delivering more for the same input.

The actual cost of quality is shown in Figure 4.4 (B); reducing errors, and thereby waste, cuts costs. The formula is very simple: reduced number of errors equals increased customer satisfaction equals improved quality. Crosby (1979) makes this point most forcibly in his book *Quality is Free*. Investment is not necessary to improve quality, managing processes is, and that involves doing the right things, i.e. ensuring conformance.

Select a short timespan, e.g. a week or a fortnight, and total the number of times within that period you have had to do each activity.

Do the same job twice	
Have work retyped	
Postpone a meeting	
Ask for clarification of a document	
Reset deadlines	
Provide 'on the spot' training	
Seek more information	
Modify printed material	
Ask for an agenda	
Clarify the purpose of a task	
Ask for work to be repeated	
Seek confirmation of a verbal agreement	
Explain documentation	
Ask for more time	
Find spare accommodation	
Confirm an order	
Change a timetable	
Duplicate information	
Get equipment repaired	
Leave a job half-finished	
Take over a delegated task	
Redefine specifications	
Return wrongly ordered goods	
'Cut corners'	
Abandon agreed procedures	

Figure 4.3 Understanding the cost of non-conformance

There is very little empirical research on waste in schools, but the figure that is often quoted for manufacturing industry in the West is 25 per cent of sales revenue. In service industries the figure may be 30 to 40 per cent of operating costs. It is difficult to speculate what such a figure might be in schools but even if it is only 10 per cent of non-staffing costs it represents a highly significant amount of money. If the principle is extended to staffing costs the implications are alarming. The following are possible areas for investigating waste:

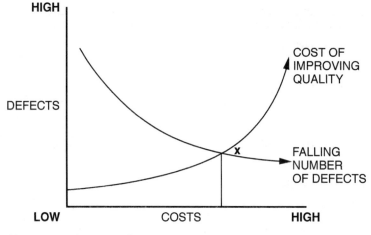

Note: x = optimum quality

(A)   Traditional view of the cost of quality

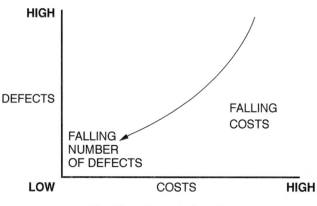

(B)   The real cost of quality

Figure 4.4 Views of the cost of quality
(*Source*: MacDonald and Piggott 1990)

- all meetings;
- INSET days, short and award bearing courses;
- inappropriate textbooks;
- under-utilised equipment;
- the stationery store;
- parents' evenings;
- photocopying;

- appointment procedures;
- the allocation of promoted posts;
- use of information technology;
- distribution of capitation;
- timetabling;
- layout of school.

Readers will be able to add their own categories and then reflect on the potential for waste. For example: an INSET day is a waste unless it leads to change, the stationery store may be full of stock that will not be used for six months – a waste of the potential of money already spent. Photocopying is necessary but teacher time spent copying is wasted. Is capitation allocated on the basis of the school development plan and the attained learning objectives or on a spurious notion of fairness? Do teachers spend hours writing out lesson notes in longhand and then have them word processed doubling the time needed to produce them?

These examples will doubtless be recognised by many and dismissed as 'the way schools are'. However, confirmation is not vindication. The cost of teacher time spent photocopying would probably amount to far more than the cost of employing a copier operator, releasing professional 'quality' time.

It may take many years to see the results of working to eliminate waste especially in the intangibles of the education process. However, there are many areas where direct benefits will be almost immediate, not least in enhanced customer satisfaction and increased commitment from those involved in the process.

Understanding variation and prevention

The greatest barrier to pupil achievement and school effectiveness is inconsistency. It is the variation in standards that causes the greatest waste in education and deviation that creates the greatest management concerns and problems. Most pupils will experience inconsistency in direct and indirect forms. Directly it will be manifested in varying standards with regard to behaviour, setting and marking homework, enforcement of standards of work etc. There is a school of thought that argues that this is inevitable and even desirable – this is, after all, what the 'real world' is like. It can only be hoped that those who advocate inconsistency in school life accept it with regard to their car being serviced, surgical procedures in hospital and the maintenance of the aircraft that will take them on holiday. Few educationalists would fly with an airline that claimed a 70 per cent reliability rate.

Two fundamental issues emerge from this point. First, no schools publish their school aims with caveats (we will be a caring community (apart from occasional cases of bullying, racism and sexism)). If promises are made (and aims are nothing but corporate promises) then systems have to be designed to keep those promises. Second, no child can wait while schools sort themselves out – all children are on short-term contracts, their timeframe is very different from that of strategic planners in schools or teachers with a full career before them to learn their craft and improve. Of course, there are many factors and variations which vitiate the achievement of consistency but the total quality school works to minimise their impact in an explicit and overt manner. The impact of variations on pupil learning is demonstrated by Hill (1996).

> *One of the more powerful conclusions arising from recent research is that it is at the class rather than the school level that the greatest variations exist. When the organisation of students in classes is taken into account, the unique variation due to schools over and above that due to differences among classes is very small indeed. . . . One of the recurring and most compelling findings within the corpus of production function research is the demonstration that how much a student learns depends on the identity of the classroom to which that student is assigned. (p. 4)*

Research in Victoria, Australia indicates that between-class differences range from 38–45 per cent for English and 53–55 per cent for Mathematics. Hill concludes:

> *It... suggests that quantum improvements in student learning can be achieved if the performance of students in all classes is brought up to the level of students in those classes in which students made the greatest progress. (p. 4)*

In other words the elimination of variation. It can be argued that variation is the greatest enemy of quality in that it represents a deviation from 'purpose' or 'requirements' – variation might be seen as professional discretion, personal idiosyncrasy or a systematic rejection of the entitlement of customers. In *Success Against the Odds* the National Commission for Education (1996) researchers found that:

> *The vision, values and goals of the school provide a rhetoric which not only gives shape to staff, pupil and parent attitudes, but also underpins organisational processes. How does this happen? As was said in relation to Selly Park: 'very little is left to chance'. Each of the successful schools endeavours to have a unified approach to the aims of the school. This often requires an explicit agreement among teachers about their aims and the implementation of policies and systems. (p. 318)*

Leaving nothing to chance and the explicit agreement are at the heart of prevention and quality assurance. The key to improvement and increased confidence that quality is being provided for every pupil all the time is the extension of best practice to every classroom. Reynolds and Stringfield (1996) have introduced the concept of the Highly Reliable School as a means of eliminating variation and so enhancing performance. The components of high reliability organisations are exactly those of using quality assurance principles. However, they are presented in a school specific context and are designed to minimise the risk of failure by focusing on particular details and taking positive action. A powerful example of this approach emerged from the investigation into the loss of the space shuttle Challenger in 1986. Richard Feynman (1993), who discovered the cause of the disaster, describes the organisational malaise that led to the disaster.

> We have also found that certification criteria used in flight readiness reviews often developed a gradually decreasing strictness. The argument that the same risk was flown before without failure is often accepted as an argument for the safety of accepting it again. Because of this, obvious weaknesses are accepted again and again – sometimes without a sufficiently serious attempt to remedy them, sometimes without a flight delay because of their continued presence. (p. 220)
>
> The Challenger flight is an excellent example: there are several references to previous flights; the acceptance and success of these flights are taken as evidence of safety. But erosion and blowby are not what the design expected. They are warnings something is wrong. The equipment is not operating as expected, and therefore there is a danger that it can operate with even wider deviations in this unexpected and not thoroughly understood way. (p. 223)

The Challenger disaster was the result of an organisational malaise: failure to observe established guidelines and practices, over-confidence about the validity of previous experience and, probably, political interference. With the exception of the latter there may be lessons for schools from this example. The failure of a child to learn is a disaster of a different order of magnitude. Importantly, though, it is one that can be avoided. The Challenger disaster could have been prevented – so can the failure of children. Reynolds and Stringfield (1996) argue that the characteristics of Highly Reliable Organisations such as air traffic control and nuclear facilities can be applied to schools:

- they have a limited range of goals which require total success. For example, the air traffic controller's job is to land the aeroplane, not to relate socially to the pilot;
- they recruit proactively and train extensively, on a pre-service and in-service basis;
- they have formalised, logical decision-making;
- they include measures to identify flows and generate changes;

- they pay considerable attention to evaluating their performance;
- they are alert to lapses and they pay attention to detail to prevent any minor error cascading into major systems failure;
- they are highly co-ordinated and interdependent;
- they are, crucially, data-rich organisations which continuously monitor how they function in order to improve their decision-making.

In practical terms the Highly Reliable Schools project has led to a number of specific strategies (as reported in the *Sunday Times*, 2 February 1997) which have achieved significant success.

- The use of reading recovery programmes.
- Systematic measurement across a range of abilities on entry into school.
- The use of individual action plans.
- The scrupulous monitoring of homework.
- The use of a computer package such as Success Maker to monitor progress.
- The introduction of coherent, systematic and consistent procedures for praise and sanction.
- Recognition and celebration of success.
- The use of mentoring and individual reviews.

All of these strategies are focused on prevention – diagnosis followed by proven corrective action. The biggest problem in assuming quality in most schools (and many other organisations) is that there is no publicly available definition of standards and no system for instituting strategies to meet those standards or for applying appropriate corrective action. If quality is to be achieved it has to be delivered and the means of achieving it made available. In essence, best practice has to be made available to all. To return to Hill's research cited earlier: in order to move the least effective classroom to the same standard as the most effective the characteristics of the latter have to be known and understood. The main reason why a learner or teacher is ineffective is probably because they have no definition of effectiveness available to them.

The principles of Highly Reliable Schools and quality assurance can be readily summarised.

Explicit definition of standards.

Consistent application of best practice procedures.

Monitoring and measurement of those procedures.

Use of remedial strategies (corrective action) when necessary.

There is nothing new in this, skilled learners and teachers engage in the process intuitively. The crucial thing in the total quality school is that everybody does it all the time. Students, as well as teachers and managers, have to accept personal responsibility for assuring the quality of what they do.

Quality standards

There is a long history of total quality approaches being supported by quality assurance strategies which are subject to external validation and accreditation. This section will outline some of those approaches and consider their applicability to schools.

BS EN ISO 9000

Most readers will be familiar with the British Standards kitemark and will probably use it as a criterion when selecting purchases. It is clear proof that a product conforms to set standards for safety, reliability and quality. In essence, the presence of the kitemark reassures the buyer that the goods are fit for the purpose intended. BS EN ISO 9000 is the kitemark for quality management systems.

BS EN ISO 9000 is not total quality management: the two are not synonymous and should not be confused. BS EN ISO 9000 is a powerful vehicle for ensuring that key organisational processes are being managed in a consistent manner and achieve conformance to a given or implied specification. The standard is used as the basis for certification of an organisation following an assessment audit carried out by an accredited third party certification body. Confirmation of the award of BS EN ISO 9000 status is subject to frequent review.

Many organisations now use the standard as the basis for managing quality systems. Its origins lie in engineering but the standard has been gradually developed so that it now covers the full range of production and service organisations. In recent years there has been growing interest in the public sector, notably the health service and further education. This is partly in response to potential employers who wish to deal with certified suppliers and partly in response to the Training Agency and Training and Enterprise Councils which are adopting quality management practices. In response to this demand the BSI has prepared guidance notes for education and training.

The factors which schools might consider in reviewing the relevance of BS EN ISO 9000 are:

1 It is increasingly becoming the 'language' of industry, commerce and the public sector.

2   Certification is a public demonstration of an organisation's commitment to quality.

3   The organisation retains full responsibility for the management processes.

4   It is 'content free', i.e. it does not prescribe what an organisation should do but rather tries to ensure consistency of delivery.

5   It provides the basis for developing quality management systems by identifying the irreducible minimum.

6   The organisation retains responsibility for setting standards and measuring performance.

BS EN ISO 9000 identifies four key factors of a quality system:

- management responsibility;
- personnel and resources;
- quality systems;
- interface with customers.

Each of these can be further broken down into their own key components.

Management responsibility

1   A quality policy which defines the key characteristics of the service to be provided.

2   Quality objectives which translate the policy into specific objectives.

3   Responsibility and authority structures to ensure that the objectives are met.

4   Management review procedures to ensure that the quality system is operating as intended.

Personnel and resources

1   Individual motivation should be recognised through selection, recognition and reward systems and by creating involvement in all aspects of work.

2   Training and development which enhances the capacity of individuals to operate quality systems.

3   Communication should be a major feature for all aspects of the organisation.

4   Resources should be provided appropriate to the specific operations required.

Quality systems

1   Quality systems should be established to control all processes. The emphasis should be on prevention.

2   Quality feedback from customers should be identified through the service quality loop.

3 Documentation should be produced including a quality manual, plan procedures and records.

4 Internal quality audits should be performed to verify the implementation and effectiveness of quality systems.

Interface with customers

1 Management should establish mechanisms to ensure responsiveness to customer needs.

2 Processes should be established to ensure effective two-way communication with customers.

This is a limited account of BS EN ISO 9000 in relation to services. Further work has been done in developing the model to apply to education and training in general and it may well be that specific work is required with regard to schools. Although the way in which the standard is expressed may be alien to many schools in fact (as argued in Chapters 3, 4 and 9) many process structures and documentation already exist in schools. It is a matter of integrating these systems to ensure consistency. A parallel may be drawn with managing a school's finances. An accounting system is essential to monitor income and expenditure, otherwise chaos would result. BS EN ISO 9000 is a structured approach to managing quality which actually simplifies and clarifies, so creating time.

BS EN ISO 9000 is not total quality; most notably it does not refer in detail to some of the crucial components of total quality:

- continuous improvement;
- leadership;
- team work;
- driving out fear;
- measurement of variation;
- breaking down barriers;
- constancy of purpose;
- vision.

This does not mean that BS EN ISO 9000 is inadequate or incomplete, rather that it needs to be set in a total quality context in order for its full potential to be realised. BS EN ISO 9000 does provide the basis for managing the system and total quality provides the context. The standard deals with the core, total quality with the intangibles – both are valid, significant and mutually supportive. Each is compromised in the absence of the other.

Healy (1994) outlines some of the benefits of using the BS EN ISO 9000 approach for a school:

An analysis was made identifying the key systems and processes that operate within the institution and are critical if the institution is to be effective. This involved tying processes down and defining... the scope, purpose, responsibility, procedure, records and performances of the systems and how they are to be monitored and evaluated. It would be one of the keys to improving quality as all staff would know:

- *exactly how a system operates;*
- *what happens and how;*
- *who is involved and responsible;*
- *how the system is monitored and evaluated. (p. 66)*

The anecdotal evidence about the use of the 9000 series in education appears to show that it can offer real benefits if developed in the context of a total quality system and not allowed to become a bureaucratic mechanism. The cost of accreditation and the work involved remains a very real issue.

Investors in People

Since its launch in 1991 Investors in People (IIP) has become one of the most popular means of a school's demonstrating its commitment to the principles of quality management. IIP is a business model concerned with all aspects of the management of people, and is a set of criteria derived from the perceived best practice of a number of highly successful business organisations.

The components of the IIP standards are:

- the existence and communication of clear organisational goals;
- commitment to a training policy to help staff achieve the goals;
- a programme of review training and development;
- evaluation of the training and development policy.

The award of the standard is administered by local Training and Enterprise Councils who employ auditors to judge the extent to which an organisation meets the national criteria. Schools which have well developed appraisal and INSET strategies have generally found the standard to be valid, relevant and attainable without excessive cost. Many schools have reported the major areas of difficulty to be linking INSET to strategic planning and the incorporation into the approval and development process of those members of staff not employed under teachers' pay and conditions.

Barker and Bell (1994) argue that Investors in People is relevant to education because it:

can give teeth to quality programmes because, undoubtedly, any commitment to the pursuit of quality by those at the top can only be achieved by a commitment to involve and develop everyone to play their part.

The challenges facing all of us in education require a fundamental change in our attitudes and actions. IIP is clearly the standard to aspire to for those schools and colleges who wish to respond to the challenges, and seize the opportunities which present themselves at the present time. (p. 173)

IIP is totally consistent with the School Teacher Appraisal Resolutions, most LEA requirements for school development planning and the OFSTED framework. The only substantial concern to be raised about the standard is that in some circumstances pupils are not seen as people – the standard needs to apply to them if they are not to be seen as the products of a school but rather as active participants in the management of their own learning.

The other major form of externally validated quality assurance is the European Quality Award which is described in detail in Chapter 2. Although it is not a quality award as such many schools would benefit from seeking the 'Crystal Mark', the award of the Plain English Society.

Education standards

It is possible to view many of the requirements of educational organisations as a means of demonstrating conformity to quality standards. The requirements of the examination boards, GNVQ etc. are specifications as are the standards set down by the legislation relating to child protection.

Three examples which illustrate many of the characteristics of accredited quality systems are now described.

The Basic Skills Agency quality mark

In 1992 the Basic Skills Agency introduced quality standards for basic skills programmes for adults. In 1995 the Agency initiated the process of developing a quality mark for secondary schools. The main elements of the quality mark for schools are:

1 A whole school action plan to improve performance in basic skills in the school.
2 An objective assessment of the need for help with basic skills in the school.
3 A target for continuous improvement of the school's performance in the basic skills.
4 An individual plan for improvement for each pupil receiving help with basic skills.
5 Regular objective assessment of the progress made by each pupil receiving help with basic skills.

6 Access to nationally recognised accreditation for each pupil receiving help with basic skills.

7 Access to training for staff involved in teaching or supporting basic skills.

8 The use of appropriate teaching and learning approaches and material to improve basic skills.

9 The involvement of parents in developing their children's basic skills.

10 An effective method for monitoring the action plan and assessing improvement in performance in basic skills.

The principles of the Basic Skills Agency are expressed as follows

> *Quality standards are essential in basic skills provision. We know that many secondary schools do more than our standards require; however these are the minimum we would expect. We want to work with schools to reduce the number of children and young people who struggle because of poor basic skills. We believe our Quality Mark can play a major part in achieving this goal.*

The work of the Basic Skills Agency is fundamentally concerned with preventing failure. The standard is a classic example of prevention through specification.

Oxford Consortium for Educational Achievement (OCEA)

Gill Bracey (1994), secretary to OCEA, describes the work of the consortium in the following way.

OCEA, The Oxford Consortium for Educational Achievement, was set up to develop Records of Achievement. The founder LEAs are Coventry, Leicestershire, Oxfordshire and Somerset, and schools and colleges from across these areas have contributed to OCEA from its inception.

Over the years, OCEA has evolved to take account of the changing national context. The Consortium is about to move into an exciting new phase, where the partnership is to include individual or groups of schools and colleges, education departments and other organisations.

Partners in the Consortium are linked by their use of the OCEA Framework of Principles for Review, Evaluation and Development. These Principles emerge from recording of achievement practice in schools and colleges across the Consortium and are now being used in a variety of educational contexts, including appraisal and school self-evaluation.

We use the Principles in two ways:

● to guide developments in the particular context to which they are being applied;

- to provide a framework for the OCEA quality assurance and improvement process, through what we call 'intervisiting'.

In OCEA, intervisiting is a formal procedure which we believe enriches self-review. The way in which the procedure has developed is characteristic of all the things OCEA does. The partners set themselves clear parameters within which to work, the process is tried out in practice, reviewed and developed, and then re-applied in the field – a cycle of continuous improvement.

In intervisiting:

- the purpose, agenda and programme for the visit are decided on by the host and agreed with the visitors;
- the programme is designed to enable the visitor to gather evidence relevant to the agenda;
- on the basis of the evidence, the visitors provide an end-of-visit review, identifying positive achievements and areas and targets for development.

In the last seven years, there have been twenty nine inter-area visits, involving heads and principals, teachers, education department officers and advisers, members of the business community, parents, TEC personnel and members of Government departments and organisations. Intervisiting is also thriving in some areas between schools, who recognise it as a supportive, developmental but rigorous way to assure and improve quality.

The intervisiting process was originally developed to provide accreditation for Records of Achievement. Recently, we have been applying the process to other educational contexts.

In March 1994, a team comprising a headteacher from Somerset, a TEC education manager, a consultant who has links with OCEA and the Director of the OCEA Management and Development Unit, spent two and a half days in Leicestershire focusing on the headteacher appraisal process. The agenda and programme for the visit were planned by Leicestershire primary and secondary headteachers and education department staff.

Evidence was gathered from discussions with about forty heads. The end-of-visit review was shared with members of the Leicestershire planning team, and the record of this review has been circulated to all those who participated in the evidence gathering discussions.

The team made observations and pointed up issues for further consideration. These will be used as a contribution to the further development of the structure and process of headteacher appraisal in Leicestershire.

This is just one practical example of the way in which OCEA framework of principles and the intervisiting process can contribute to quality assurance and improvement. In fact, we would argue that a principled approach actually provides the key to coherence in all issues related to quality development. The translation of the OCEA principles into the management of quality in a school can be seen in the following statement taken from the Principles and Policies document of Thomas Estley Community College, Leicestershire:

Principles into Practice

The OCEA Framework of Principles is used by the college, as a learning community, to prove and improve continuously the quality of its practice in teaching and learning.

Evaluation, review and development in the learning community of the College take place within and against the principles.

Hence, the principles guide the processes of TEACHING and LEARNING *and* provide the focus for REVIEW and QUALITY IMPROVEMENT. In essence, they form a learning policy for the whole College.

1. We recognise and actively encourage learning, achievement and development in a range of contexts.

2. We involve all participants in the planning, delivery and review of learning.

3. We provide opportunities for the development and practice of skills which encourage individual responsibility for learning.

4. We share with learners criteria for achievement.

5. We develop reviewing and recording processes to inform progress and future learning.

6. We provide opportunities for learners to compile a summary record of their progress and achievements.

7. We support the continuity and progression of learning.

8. We invite an external contribution as part of the review process.

9. We use these principles as a basis for the evaluation, review and development of professional practice.

The OCEA Framework of Principles supports and sustains the realisation and implementation of LIFELONG LEARNING.

The Office for Standards in Education

OFSTED's mission is 'Improvement through Inspection' – this is a direct contradiction of the total quality axiom 'Quality cannot be inspected in'. The OFSTED framework and inspection process form the basis of most schools' work in raising standards. In the context of a discussion about total quality three concerns have to be raised about the OFSTED process:

1　It is an historic process (rather than preventative) and occurs at widely spaced intervals.

2　The criteria are imposed rather than being developed internally and the evidential base for judgements is problematic.

3　The cost may be disproportionate to the benefits.

There is no doubt that the OFSTED process is fundamentally important in terms of accountability; however, in terms of continuous improvement it may serve to sustain a dependency culture inhibiting creative and holistic school-based responses to the problem of increasing confidence that customer needs are being met all the time.

Summary

- Managing quality is about prevention.
- All work is a process.
- Managing processes is about adding value and eliminating waste.
- Processes in schools can be managed.
- Prevention requires specification, measurement and corrective action.
- Improving quality means reducing failure.
- Variation is the enemy of quality.
- The key management task is to manage variables.
- A range of standards to help with quality assurance is available.

Action

1　Understand the cost of failure.
2　Switch from inspection to prevention.
3　Make everyone responsible for preventing failure.

5

■ ■ ■

Mission and Planning

Introduction

Virtually all schools will have published a set of aims, statements about the values and principles which are the basis of the school's working life. The aims may be published in the 'Handbook for Staff' or the 'School Prospectus'. Some schools may also publish an accompanying list of objectives, but these are often indistinguishable from the aims.

Analysis of a school's aims will usually reveal entirely proper, appropriate and valid sentiments. However, in the context of quality management a number of questions have to be asked about the traditional approach to aims and their relationship to planning.

- Who wrote the aims?
- When were they written?
- When were they last revised?
- Do all those affected know and accept them?
- Are they used as criteria for evaluation?
- Do they inform all management processes?
- Are they written in meaningful language?
- Is any attempt made to measure the extent to which they are achieved?

This leads to the first issue to be considered when approaching this topic – that of nomenclature. On the one hand it doesn't really matter as aims, mission statement, vision statement, statement of purpose etc. can all describe the same piece of text. On the other, there may be some virtue in signalling a change in the school's way of thinking and working by changing the terminology. Mission statement for instance also conveys an appropriate sense of purpose.

It is, however, equally valid to think in terms of the school's promises. Indeed it could be argued that the whole purpose of total quality is to keep the promises made in such a statement. What is important is to avoid the feeling of imposed 'management-speak' or the adoption of an alien and inappropriate language.

Mission

Successful schools have explicit values shared by all members of the school community, explained to all those who come into contact with the school, and used as the basis for all aspects of the life of the school. Successful schools know where they are going and how they are going to get there. Values which are implicit are not capable of implementation. There is therefore a need to translate the values which inform the management of a school into a public and shared statement which is a public commitment to the core purpose. Such a statement is usually referred to as the mission.

The mission statement serves a number of practical purposes.

- It characterises the school to its community.
- It provides a sense of direction and purpose.
- It serves as a criterion for policy-making.
- It sets the school culture.
- It generates consistency of action.
- It identifies clients.
- It serves to motivate and challenge.

Above all the mission statement creates a sense of uniqueness and identity which serves as a platform for action. A mission statement has the function of a motto or badge – it is a label which is instantly recognisable and sends an unequivocal comment about values and purposes. The mission statement equally indicates what the school wants to succeed in; what it does and does not do and, crucially, how it seeks to do it. It becomes possible then to apply an instant test of validity and relevance to any proposed change: to what extent is this proposed change consistent with our core purpose? A mission statement makes explicit the values of a school and therefore does much to indicate the expectations as to what the culture of the school should be. This in turn facilitates the development of operating procedures that translate principles into practice. Mission statements inform the writing of objectives which will inform budgetary planning, staff development and curriculum planning. Equally they set the context for the writing of management procedures, job descriptions, schemes of work etc. By relating these means of implementation back to the mission statement, consistency is possible. The statement also needs to specify clients so that the responsibility to provide a quality service is a permanent feature of activity in the school.

Finally, mission statements are about challenge, excitement and giving meaning to work. They help to set the routine, the mundane and the ordinary in the context of the broader purpose and the drive for continuous improvement.

If the mission statement is to be more than a series of clichés, or even worse, marginal to the life of the school, it has to be rooted in a number of fundamental components. These are expressed in Figure 5.1.

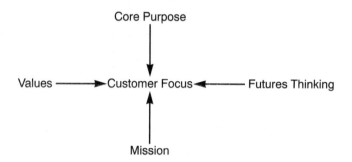

Figure 5.1 Fundamental components of the mission statement

The core purpose is the fundamental issue to be decided and articulated; it is the a priori on which everything else is posited. Surprisingly few schools are clear and confident about what their core purpose is, or it exists only by extrapolation from practice. Thus for many schools the core purpose would appear to be to allow teaching to take place and to deliver the National Curriculum. For another school it might be the achievement of academic excellence and for another to provide the only safe and secure environment in a child's life. All are valid but need to be made explicit if the school is to be consistent.

Whatever a school identifies as its core purpose the central element is likely to focus in some way on the learning process. It may well be that one of the most important outcomes of reviewing a school's mission is a debate about the nature and purpose of learning. Debate about the core purpose will create the axioms that will inform every subsequent decision and also create the 'mindscapes' that are fundamental to leadership behaviour and the creation of an organisational culture. Schools are often coy about the status of learning, largely because it is so complex a topic and the articulation of core purpose is often in terms of teaching and the curriculum which are easier to describe. Equally elusive is the characterisation of what 'caring community' or effective social relationships' actually mean.

The debate about the core purpose can help to create a vocabulary which will enhance understanding of the key determinant of every other aspect of the school. Few commercial organisations are successful if they see their core purpose as making a profit. It is usually expressed in terms of quality service or customer satisfaction, and profit follows from these.

Values are equally difficult and elusive and often not articulated. If the core purpose is what the school is about then values are how it is to be. There is a danger in assuming some sort of moral hegemony and taking values for granted. While it is highly unlikely that any school would wish to depart from the broad consensual view of the society in which it operates it is important that the priorities are clear and explicit and that the ethical basis for the decision-making process is unambiguous. Schools are fundamentally moral communities; there are no value-free decisions to be taken. Equally the potential for leadership, as opposed to management, is significantly enhanced. For Sergiovanni (1992):

> *When purpose, social contract and local school autonomy become the basis of schooling, two important things happen. The school is transformed from an organisation to a covenantal community, and the basis of authority changes, from an emphasis on bureaucratic and psychological authority to moral authority ... the school changes ... from a mere instrument designed to achieve certain ends to a virtuous enterprise. (p. 102)*

It is difficult to see how any process in a school can have integrity unless it has a clear lineage back to agreed values and this in turn assumes a sophisticated level of discourse throughout the school community.

Futures thinking develops the issues raised in Chapter 1 about the changing context in which schools are having to operate. While the core purpose and values may be abiding, although both may have to be reinterpreted, the environment in which they are to be applied will undoubtedly change. The important feature of futures thinking is to avoid a short-term approach or incremental planning and

> *to use futures thinking in order to develop a vision about a desired future state and then to plan backwards from that state. (Davies and Ellison 1997, p. 76)*

The vision of the school in the future is not an idealised dream but rather a description of how the school will be on the basis of the best possible understanding of the environmental forces that will shape it.

In essence the core purpose, values and futures thinking help to describe the destination of the school as currently understood. Most journeys are enhanced if there is a destination specified. However, the nature of the journey has to take

81

into account the needs of the 'passengers'. Hence the need for a customer focus. The application of the other three variables could produce a mission statement that made schools wonderful places to be a teacher in or schools that had a servile response to government policy-making – losing the professional dimension in the formulation of the nature of schools and the components of the pedagogic process. The issue of 'Who is the customer?' is dealt with in detail in Chapter 3. However, in the context of the mission statement it is difficult to conceptualise any group other than children. It is vital that other groups involved in the school, notably parents and all the staff, are not forgotten but there is a real need to state the primacy of children in the school. An interesting issue here is the way in which 'adults other than teachers' are described and referred to. 'Non-teaching' has all sorts of interesting connotations in terms of perceived significance and moral value.

The process of producing a mission statement is as significant as the statement itself. The level of involvement, consultation and shared decision-making will do much to make the statement operative. It is equally important that the process should reflect the principles outlined in the statement. In essence, the greater the involvement the higher the quality of the statement and the greater the potential commitment. *Ex cathedra* statements which are handed down are unlikely to function as the source of vision and motivation.

However, vision by committee seems as unlikely to work, so considerable care has to be exercised in managing the process of developing a mission statement. There are three main stages to producing a mission statement: planning, writing and reviewing. Each stage is time consuming, intellectually demanding and requires significant skills of team work and collaborative decision-making and problem-solving. Writing a mission statement is thus both an essential prerequisite to implementing a quality management policy and an example of such a process. The natural focus for initiating and sustaining the process is the senior management team. However, the impact of a mission statement is directly related to the involvement of those it will affect and those who will have to implement it. The use of a project team approach may well be the most appropriate.

Planning the statement

Preparation for the production of a mission statement is essential as failure may be more counterproductive than never starting. The issues to be considered by senior managers can be best expressed in a series of questions.

1 Does the current situation demand a fundamental reappraisal of the school's values?
2 Do the benefits of a mission statement justify the time and energy required?
3 Will what we do make a real difference?

4 Is there something important to be said about our values and practices that will influence the future of the school?

5 Can we afford to invest the time?

6 Can we afford not to invest the time?

7 How objective and honest can we be about our management practices and relationships?

8 Are we prepared to seek and accept feedback from all our clients?

9 Do we have the skills necessary to initiate and sustain the process?

10 Are we prepared to implement, work by and be judged by the statement we produce?

Unless the answers to these questions are unequivocal, it may well be that there are other issues to be considered first. In the case of a senior management team it could be that a process of systematic team building is necessary (see Chapter 8). Equally significant is the perception of the headteacher. Unless she or he has formulated a clear view of her/his personal expectations and values and is able and willing to communicate them to maximum effect then the process of developing a mission statement will not work.

The second stage of the planning process is to establish the context that will inform the implementation of the mission statement. This is a complex process of identification, clarification and prioritisation which may well require use of the techniques outlined in Chapter 3. The variables to be considered will change from school to school but may include:

- statutory requirements, notably the demands of the Education Reform Act 1988 and associated legislation;
- LEA policies and procedures;
- the views of children, parents and employers;
- the views of the governing body;
- the perspectives of all staff;
- the views of LEA advisers, officers and others with whom the school has regular dealings;
- documentary evidence:
  - inspection reports;
  - whole school review (e.g. GRIDS and DION);
  - evaluation and monitoring reports;
  - reports to the governing body;
  - statistical data.

These data will do much to identify current views and attitudes, needs and expectations. However, a mission statement should not simply be descriptive but should also be concerned with building on success. This requires articulating the vision, and can be done in a number of ways.

1 Celebrating strengths – each person involved is asked to identify the strengths of the school, the aspects of its work and life that are most worthy of recognition and celebration and then to specify the factors which contribute to the success.

2 Envisioning – individuals are asked to envision the ideal state for the school in five or ten years' time. What sort of place should the school be? How should it feel?

3 Client orientation – members of the project team complete the phrases: 'If I were a parent considering sending my child to this school I would want. . .'. 'If I were a child at this school I would want. . .'.

4 Clarifying values – 'In this school we really care about. . .'.

Each of these exercises generates a range of values and principles that are essentially personal. However, this reflects the reality of any organisation – it is the sum of individual perceptions. The important thing is to aggregate these individual perceptions so that they are shared and refined into a collective view, i.e. the highest common denominator. Significant and fundamental as these views and values are, they need to be set in the context of anticipated and known changes which will influence the school – what might be termed the 'hard' data.

- What are the demographic trends influencing the school's recruitment?
- What impact will the implementation of the National Curriculum have?
- How will the continuing implementation of LMS influence the school's resource base?
- What are the likely future needs of other schools, higher and further education and employers?
- What is the age and qualifications profile of the staff of the school? How will this affect curriculum provision?
- Do we have any identifiable weakness to redress?
- How appropriate are training and development strategies for staff?
- Are management structures and procedures appropriate?

The clarification of values and expectations coupled with analysis of the context in which the schools will be operating provide the raw data for the production of the mission statement. The statement is then a valid basis for the writing of a development plan. The relationship is shown in Figure 5.2.

Writing the statement

Once all values and expectations have been expressed and collected, and as many data have been collected as are available, it is then possible to write the

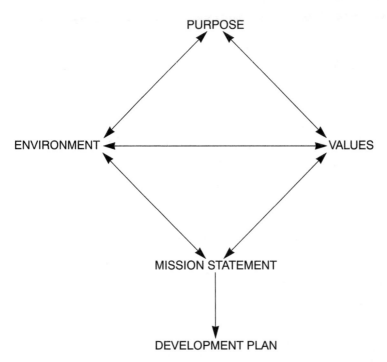

PURPOSE

ENVIRONMENT

VALUES

MISSION STATEMENT

DEVELOPMENT PLAN

Figure 5.2 Mission and strategy

mission statement. There are two issues to be considered in the writing process: first, it is a complex process involving significant skills in synthesising complex issues and adopting appropriate language. The quality of 'conformity to requirements' is particularly apposite here – the person who is going to use the document, and for what purposes, should determine its language and layout. It should not be seen as an opportunity for intellectual 'one-upmanship' but rather as a real, relevant and usable document. Second, the actual writing process needs to be carefully managed so as to ensure commitment and enhance relationships.

There is a tension between the practical demands of producing the statement and ensuring maximum involvement and creativity. No committee has yet written a sonnet. The writing process is probably best handled by the project team with a consultant/facilitator. The role of the consultant is to help achieve a product in a reasonable timescale while questioning, checking and reminding the team of its task and the context in which it is operating.

Once a first draft is produced it can be tested by the team using the following checklists:

Process

1 Were you able to make a full contribution?
2 Were you listened to?
3 Did anyone in the team block your ideas?
4 Was the team creative?
5 Was the team realistic?
6 Did the team hold onto the core purpose of the school?
7 Has the team resolved ambiguities and uncertainties?
8 Are you personally fully committed to the mission statement?

Outcome

Your mission statement will not work if it is:

- written in an alien language;
- a series of pious aspirations;
- a list of outcomes;
- a series of imperatives to staff;
- insensitive to clients' needs
- too general;
- too prescriptive;
- reinforcing the status quo;
- set in a short timescale;
- reactive and pragmatic;
- lacking leadership commitment.

Assuming that the statement passes the above 'tests' then it should be shown to a cross-section of those whom it is going to affect. They could be asked to comment on its clarity and realism, its comprehensiveness, its acceptability and applicability. Negative responses indicate more work to be done. Positive responses serve as the basis for publication, dissemination and explanation.

Although a model of a generic statement is offered (p. 89) it is important to stress the unique nature of the mission statement for each school. A number of examples are provided, not as prescriptions of good practice but rather to illustrate the range and diversity of what might constitute a mission statement

Murphy (1997, p. 139) provides the mission statement for St Edward's School in Poole, a joint Roman Catholic/Church of England school.

Jesus says 'Where people come together in my name,
I am with them.'
Matthew 18:20

As a Christian learning community which promotes the value of family life, we support the parents as primary educators of their children. We challenge every student to strive for the highest standard of personal, social and intellectual development, and aim for excellence in all they do. We recognise that all children are unique and aim to guide them along their personal Journey of Faith. During the day-to-day life of our school and in all aspects of the curriculum we promote Gospel values.

We provide opportunities for every member of our community to experience prayer, worship and reflection.

My commandment is this: *Love one another just as I love you.*
John 15:12

This is a clear exemplification of core purpose ('a Christian community') founded on Christian values and with a clear sense of how the school is to be. Significantly the school has taken two phrases from the full mission statement 'learning together' and 'aiming for excellence' as slogans to help everyone translate the mission into everyday use.

Tribus (1994) cites the mission statement for Mt Edgecumbe High School in Sitka, Alaska, the first school in the world to work systematically towards total quality. The school's mission statement includes the following commitments:

Mt Edgecumbe High School is a paradigm shift in philosophy to the usual school programme. Each curricular area offers innovative teaching methods that not only enhance opportunities for Mt Edgecumbe High School students, but serve as models for other schools.

... Programme and curriculum are based upon a conviction that students have a great and often unrealised potential.

Administrators, teachers and other staff are required to keep current on educational advances and to initiate innovative, challenging and stimulating classroom programmes and activities.

Teachers and staff analyse issues to anticipate future social and economic needs of Alaska, such as Alaska's economic position among the Pacific Rim nations....

Mt Edgecumbe's mission statement is about 400 words long. Haggerston School's by comparison is just seven. (Collarbone 1997, p. 23)

A ttendence

C ommitment

H omework

I mprove

E ffort

V alue

E veryone

Both are valid and appropriate; the 'correctness' of a mission statement is determined by the extent to which it has meaning within its specific context.

What is important is that apart from the various criteria discussed in this chapter the mission statement should be compelling as shown in this example.

Our Mission is to be:

Committed to Excellence

Pioneers and Leaders in Education

In describing the mission statement for King Harold Grant Maintained School, Waltham Abbey, Healy (1994) describes how the mission statement is supported by vision statements that are taken by teams and translated into specific, short-term targets. The vision statements

> *are critical within the quality improvement process as they form the backcloth, the frame within which teams root their work. (p. 63)*

What is important is that the statement should be understandable to those to whom it applies, the children. Equally it should be capable of being used by them. How many of the people in your school community know the school's mission statement and are able to demonstrate how what they are doing at any given moment is an exemplification of that statement?

Reviewing the statement

Once the mission statement has been published and is a fundamental component of school planning and decision-making, its validity will be tested frequently. A review of the school's mission will therefore be a part of all monitoring, inspection and evaluation procedures. However, changes in environmental factors operating on the school may also necessitate a review of the continuing validity of the statement. Although the central purpose of the school may be immutable, the means by which that purpose is achieved will, of necessity, have to be modified. If a mission statement is found to be seriously deficient, is not being used to inform management activity or is irrelevant to the working life of the school then it is probably not a mission statement at all, but rather the views of a minority which have not been made part of the school culture.

The best test of a mission statement is the extent to which it permeates all aspects of school management, how far it becomes the working language of the school and the quality benchmark for all individuals and teams to review their work.

The example of a possible mission statement shown in Figure 5.3 is not intended to be prescriptive but rather to illustrate how the various components

---

MISSION STATEMENT OF XYZ SCHOOL

1 Our primary purpose is to enhance children's quality of learning through the effective and efficient delivery of the curriculum.

2 We believe that our first responsibility is to our clients, to meet their needs and to provide outstanding service.

3 We will provide a range of educational and social experiences appropriate to the age, ability and needs of our pupils.

4 We will have consistently high expectations and match these with high-quality resources and learning strategies.

5 We are committed to honesty and responsibility in all relationships, respecting the legitimate rights of individuals and stressing the importance of social awareness and sensitivity.

6 We will create opportunities for every individual in the school community to develop her or his maximum potential.

7 We will manage resources to ensure maximum educational benefit.

8 We will create and sustain a professional learning environment.

9 We will adopt a philosophy of continuous improvement of every aspect of the school's work and life.

Figure 5.3 A model mission statement

identified earlier might be expressed. It cannot be stressed too strongly that each mission statement must be unique to its school and that the process of producing the statement is a significant event in the implementation of a total quality approach.

Planning

If the mission statement identifies the destination of a school, then planning is necessary to specify the timetable and stops on the journey. No school will achieve quality management through rhetoric and exhortation; values are only given reality through action, and managing is about action rather than contemplation. A mission statement is therefore only valid when it is part of a planning process which translates aspirations into activity and helps each individual see her/his actions contribute to the attainment of the school's purposes. Planning therefore has to integrate the mission statement into a process which allows individuals to plan and prioritise their own work so that school needs and individual activity are harmonised.

The key process in Figure 5.4 is vectoring – moving from the general to the specific, the abstract to the concrete, the common to the personal. It is only when individuals are able to participate in the setting of specific targets that measurable outcomes will occur.

MISSION STATEMENT

OBJECTIVES

TARGETS

Figure 5.4 Mission and planning

In the hierarchy shown in Figure 5.4 objectives are short-term (one or two year) school priorities and targets are personal, short-term (six months to one year) outcomes. School objectives are established through the development planning process and targets through the appraisal process. The interconnection of mission statement, development planning and target setting is demonstrated in Figure 5.5.

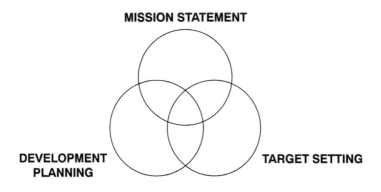

Figure 5.5 Mission, planning and targets

In this process each component feeds off the other, they are interdependent and inadequacy on the part of one will compromise the other two. At the critical point where the three coincide there is quality in action with values directly influencing behaviour.

Development planning

The planning cycle, in any of its various formulations, is now widely known. However, it is important to stress in the context of quality management that the planning process has to be client driven and that the management of the cycle is, in itself, a significant quality issue. This places the mission statement firmly at the outset of the planning process and requires constant reference to it as the criterion for acceptability and prioritisation. Equally important is that the planning cycle harmonises all components of the management process. Thus the mission statement informs and drives curriculum planning, which in turn informs staff recruitment, deployment and development, which then determines the budget. The budgetary process is therefore objective driven rather than being incremental and the quality purpose of the school is the key determinant of decision-making.

Principal stages in the planning process may be readily identified.

- **Setting objectives:** translating the broad imperatives of the mission statement into specific outcomes which are attributed to individuals, set within a defined timescale and with clear performance indicators.

- **Allocating resources:** ensuring that financial, physical and personal resources are attributed to each objective so as to ensure that it is attainable. There is no merit in setting objectives without allocating the necessary resources. Equally important is deployment of staff with appropriate skills, knowledge and authority.

- **Implementation:** this requires translation of objectives into specific actions by individuals. For this to happen these actions need to be defined in concrete terms with appropriate training and development if necessary. Implementation may be by individuals or through teams.

- **Monitoring and evaluation:** if objectives have been appropriately written then monitoring is a simple exercise; if performance indicators are written in sufficiently concrete and specific terms then failure or success will be immediately apparent. Evaluation is carried out in the terms of the mission statement, i.e. the extent to which the objectives have enhanced compliance with stated purposes.

Appraisal and target setting

Appraisal is a fundamentally significant process in the context of quality management. Appraisal of managers and teachers in schools may be said to have three essential purposes.

1 Recognition and reinforcement of success and consolidation of effective practice.

2 Diagnosis of professional development and training needs.

3 Negotiation of personal targets which identify personal responsibility for the implementation of school objectives.

Appraisal as envisaged by the National Steering Group (DES, 1989) and the DES in Circular 12/91 (1991) is operated in a hierarchical way. Thus at each stage of the school hierarchy there is a clear responsibility to translate the school's mission and objectives into practical outcomes which lead to change.

How the appraisal process might operate

Focus from mission statement

We will have consistently high expectations and match these with high-quality resources and learning strategies.

School objective 1997/98

To reduce unwarranted absence in year 11 by 50 per cent in the current academic year.

Deputy headteacher's target

To review learning resources and teaching strategies and organise the production of appropriate materials for less able students in year 11 and implement changes by January 1998.

Classroom teacher's target

To attend the LEA course on 'History for the less able', to present proposals at the following departmental meeting and to contribute to the production of flexible learning materials.

Outcome of the appraisal process

At each stage the target becomes more specific and the whole process is underpinned by:

- the allocation of appropriate resources of time, money etc.;
- the provision of appropriate training;
- the existence of clear criteria for acceptable performance.

The aspiration of the mission statement is thus turned into concrete behaviour, the impact of which can be measured and modified if appropriate. By following this process, roles and responsibilities are also clarified and the workload of individuals is managed more effectively. However, the process will only work if the mission statement exists, is written in appropriate terms, has the commitment of all involved and is a living document used at all stages of the management process. Without an integrated approach aims are likely to remain pious platitudes, and planning ad hoc and reactive.

Summary

- Quality management requires a mission statement which permeates all aspects of school life.
- The mission statement must be orientated towards the school's clients.
- The mission statement must be understandable, specific and capable of implementation.
- The production of a mission statement is the responsibility of senior management.
- The statement must balance vision with realism.
- A mission statement must be written for its audience – not its writers.
- The statement must be constantly communicated. Planning must grow out of the mission.
- Appraisal is a vehicle for translating principle into practice.

Action

1 Review your school aims – do they directly influence your management processes?

2 Do your school aims provide a vivid and exciting picture of what your school is all about? If not where does the vision come from?

3 Refer to your aims/mission every day. Make them real for all members of the school community.

4 Find out if your colleagues' vision is compatible with yours.

5 Does your conduct reinforce your school's values?

6

■ ■ ■

Culture

Introduction

Culture is one of the least tangible but most significant elements in creating a quality environment. If the culture of a school is not appropriate then the principles outlined in Chapters 2, 3 and 5 will have limited impact and the practical approaches in Chapters 7, 8 and 9 will become superficial rituals. This chapter is therefore a bridge between principles and application. The cultures of schools vary enormously and have a profound and direct impact upon behaviour and performance. The purpose of this chapter is to identify the factors that contribute to a school's culture and the changes that may be necessary to create a 'quality culture'. The following issues are examined:

- defining culture;
- defining a quality culture;
- factors influencing culture;
- creating a total quality learning culture.

Defining culture

In simplistic terms an organisation's culture is its personality – the sum of all those elements that add up to make it unique. Culture is the product of the shared values, beliefs, priorities, expectations and norms that serve to inform the way in which an organisation manifests itself to the world. Culture only has meaning when it is given expression and when that expression is in tangible forms. The critical point about culture is that it is constructed from those abstractions which are shared, those which are widely held and dominant. All organisations have multiple sub-sets, localised beliefs which give meaning to particular parts of the whole; however, in the context of quality there needs to be a consistency of purpose, a shared value system which permeates all aspects of organisation and so is manifested in practical terms. There is an obvious tension between the demands of the organisation and the values of the individual. The image of quality management is often a distorted one of uniformity and conformity. The skill in managing cultural change is to generate consensus, to recruit and develop in accordance with the culture and to help those who cannot 'fit' to find an appropriate niche so that they too are fully developed in personal terms.

Describing, defining and illustrating the concept of culture

Charles Handy (1990) has gone further than most to make the issues clear and understandable. Handy has developed the notion of tribes to help define the characteristics that go to make up organisations.

Handy's organisational tribes

Figure 6.1 provides a limited summary of Handy's detailed discussion. However, it should be possible to identify schools that conform to each of the tribal definitions. It is possible to caricature schools: the 'club' school with the dominant and all-pervasive headteacher; the 'role' school, the large comprehensive; the 'task' school, often a primary or middle school; and the 'person' school, the traditional grammar. In reality of course all schools will contain elements of each tribe. In the secondary school different departments will display different tribal characteristics: the role-based science department, the task-based English department, the person-based art department and the club-based PE department.

The issue to be discussed is which of these tribes is appropriate to the quality organisation. The answer is probably not one of them in isolation; all contain elements that are valid. The emphasis on leadership, systems, team work, task focus and high responsiveness all conform to quality criteria. However, this is too random and haphazard so a fifth tribe has been added, with due deference to Professor Handy.

The customer tribe is symbolised by the chain for the tribe only has meaning when it is linked to its suppliers and customers. The focus is totally on the customer since everyone is a customer. Communication is open and two-way and the tribe is motivated by its shared value system. Its responsiveness is total, it only exists to delight its customers. The customer tribe is unusual in that it has invariably evolved from one of the other tribes and traces of earlier behaviour often emerge. However, the tribe is determined to establish itself in its own right.

Handy also uses the metaphor of classical gods to help analyse the individual's understanding of organisational culture.

	CLUB	ROLE	TASK	PERSON	CUSTOMER
STRUCTURE	SPIDER'S WEB	PYRAMID	NET	CLUSTER OR CONSTELLATION	CHAIN
FOCUS	THE LEADER	THE STRUCTURE	THE TEAM	THE PERSON	THE CUSTOMER
COMMUNICATION	BASED ON TRUST SHARED UNDERSTANDING	FORMAL BASED ON SYSTEMS AND PROCEDURES	OPEN, RELAXED	PERSONAL	OPEN, TWO-WAY
STYLE	PERSONALITY CENTRED HOMOGENEOUS	PREDICTABLE, CERTAIN	CO-OPERATIVE FORWARD LOOOKING	TECHNICALLY BASED	OBSESSIVE, VALUE-DRIVEN, MEASURED
RESPONSIVENESS	RAPID FLEXIBLE	LIMITED, RULE-CENTRED	TASK-FOCUSED	HIGH	HIGH CONSTANT IMPROVEMENT
EXAMPLES	ARTISTS THEATRE POLITICS	GOVERNMENT DEPARTMENTS	SURGICAL TEAMS PROJECT GROUPS	DOCTORS BARRISTERS ARCHITECTS UNIVERSITY DEPARTMENTS	ANY TEAM COMPANY OR ORGANISATION

Figure 6.1 Handy's organisational tribes

97

- Zeus works through people by power, operates by strength of personality.
- Apollo works through harmony and logic, values structure and security.
- Athena works through excitement, energy, problem-solving and teams.
- Dionysus, the free spirit, loyal to the craft, intolerant of organisations.

To this distinguished pantheon it is proposed to add Themis. She offered wise counsel to the other gods, was always helpful and obliging; the goddess of wisdom and justice, she could also envisage the future. In these respects she seems ideal as a goddess of quality, especially as she was also revered as a counsellor and a guide for public debate.

Handy's insights provide powerful clues to the components of an organisation's culture. These have been identified in Figure 6.1 as structure, focus, communication, style and responsiveness. Each of these will be significant in its own right; together they will have a profound impact upon the way an organisation actually works as opposed to the intentions or wishes of its leaders and managers. However, to understand the practical implications of managing a quality culture it is necessary to translate these conceptual models into the practical aspects of managing in schools. Central to the creation and maintenance of a culture are mission, leadership and teams (dealt with in Chapters 5, 7 and 8 respectively). It is not proposed to repeat the issues identified in these chapters but rather to show how they impact on routine procedures.

Defining a quality culture

If culture is the personality of an organisation then a quality school is restless, constantly questioning, never satisfied, challenging norms and believing that things can always be better. Quality management requires a belief in an infinite capacity for improvement of organisations, processes and people. It is difficult to think of a better environment for such an approach than a school. Schools manage the most complex process of continuous improvement – the growth of children's learning.

Figure 6.1 identified five components of an organisation's culture. The central theme of a quality culture is continuous improvement: the organisation is totally committed to improving all aspects of every activity. There is never a time when there is nothing to be improved; everything is capable of further refinement, further reduction of error and greater customer satisfaction. This approach can manifest itself in terms of the five components.

Structure

The most powerful image is that of the chain – indeed total quality is often defined as a 'chain of customers'. The image conveys a crucial message of interdependence, the chain being only as strong as the weakest link and having meaning only when the links are firmly interconnected. Quality is integrated into all aspects of the organisation; it permeates every process. Quality management is management, not any other activity.

Focus

There is an unequivocal recognition that the organisation exists to serve the customer; it has no other justification. This view is extended to internal and external customers with an emphasis on the external, meaning that everyone accepts the responsibility for providing outstanding service and that the primary purpose of each job is customer satisfaction. This is managed by constant feedback and measurement.

Communication

Quality organisations give priority to high-quality communication, stressing the importance of a constant two-way dialogue. Communication is open, frank and purposeful. This is most powerfully demonstrated in the use of autonomous teams which have highly sophisticated internal communication and are able to talk to other teams to direct effect.

Style

The quality organisation is driven by values, not pragmatism or expediency. A long-term view is taken with an emphasis on measurement to monitor progress. Crucially, everyone in the organisation is obsessed with quality – it permeates language, working procedures and is the criterion used in every activity. High expectations are the norm and are made explicit.

Responsiveness

'The customer is always right' is a cliché but it is one that drives quality organisations: meeting customer needs, as they are expressed, is what the organisation exists to do. The emphasis is on prevention not inspection, on delighting the customer by providing superior service and on continuous improvement. A customer complaint triggers action, not resentment or avoidance.

Central to these factors is the behaviour of the leadership of an organisation. For schools to create a quality culture, senior staff must be permanently obsessed with quality. The culture of the school will be a reflection of the head and senior managers and this must be manifested in behaviour, language and imagery. No example of poor quality is ever ignored, all communications refer to quality and all encounters are viewed in terms of their potential to advance quality. However, schools cannot operate by exhortation – the culture of quality needs to permeate all aspects of management processes and practical examples are outlined in the next section.

Factors influencing culture

When anthropologists study a society they derive their conclusions about its culture from observed behaviour. Social behaviour is the means by which culture is most powerfully transmitted: do as I say or do as I do. Creating a culture appropriate to quality management implies a focus on specifics, tangible expressions which communicate meaning. In many industrial organisations the first tangible results of a total quality approach have been the abolition of reserved parking spaces, the merging of the executive dining room with the management restaurant and the works canteen and everybody or nobody clocking in. These are changes that send a direct and uncomplicated message – quality means change in every aspect of working life. More important, the values and mission of the organisation are translated into tangibles which help change understanding and create a new language, new myths and symbols and a view of the reality of the organisation.

Because schools are so diverse and because there can be no stereotype of what makes a 'quality' school the factors influencing quality have to be understood in the specific context of the individual school. The following factors are intended to be generic, but the components of each factor must be identified and determined by each school. Unless they are specific to an individual school, i.e. derived from its mission statement and generated by those working in the school, they are unlikely to be either valid or capable of implementation. The issues to be considered in such an approach might include:

- Values and mission – the extent to which these are public, shared, understood and acted on.
- Organisational structure – the logic behind the school's hierarchy, the way in which responsibilities are shared with possible duplication of responsibility.
- Communication – the effectiveness of communication within and between work groups and individuals, the quality of information flow.
- Decision-making – the amount of real delegation, the quality of decisions, the levels of involvement.

- Working environment – the standards of comfort, cleanliness and suitability for teaching, learning and social interaction.

- Recruitment and selection – the use of appropriate techniques to match people to the culture of the school and the skills required to do the job.

- Curriculum planning – the timetable, deployment of staff, access to teaching resources.

- Budget and resource management – the extent to which the budget is driven by the curriculum, perceived equity in the allocation of capitation, the availability of resources.

- Pastoral care and discipline – the perceived effectiveness and fairness of pastoral systems.

- Community – the quality of relationships with governors, parents, business, local authorities etc.

An essential precursor to the implementation of a total quality approach is an understanding of the prevailing culture. Attitudinal change will be the foundation of any significant modification of organisational culture; equally the imposition of an 'alien' culture is doomed to failure. A culture 'review' is an essential precursor for two reasons: first, it provides accurate data for managing the implementation process; second, it identifies the priorities for action. Figure 6.2 illustrates a school culture review. (It can also inform forcefield analysis and readiness and capability techniques – see Chapter 10.)

As with all such activities completing the review in isolation may provide insight but is bound to be limited in its potential for action. Aggregating the scores of all interested parties will provide a more powerful basis for analysis, and then using the review as the basis for team meetings and sharing perceptions which are then translated into actions has the potential to bring about real cultural change. The other chapters of this book all provide insights into the practical aspects of creating a quality culture. Examples of some of the other issues are now examined

Organisational structure

Chapter 8 places great emphasis on the team as a crucial component of total quality management. Indeed the team and quality are symbiotic. In planning the implementation of a quality management approach the structure of a school needs to be reviewed in the light of the answers to the following questions:

- To what extent does the structure facilitate the functioning of autonomous teams?

- Does the structure reinforce the principles of real and effective delegation?

- How far is the structure a reflection of the school's values and how far an historic, bureaucratic legacy?

Indicate where you perceive your school to be on each continuum:

1.	Values not shared, rarely discussed	1 2 3 4 5	Values real, shared, used
2.	Leaders concerned with procedures	1 2 3 4 5	Leaders involved with people
3.	Complaints a nuisance	1 2 3 4 5	Complaints the basis of growth
4.	Unclear procedures	1 2 3 4 5	Defined processes
5.	Groups with little sense of purpose	1 2 3 4 5	Self-managing teams
6.	Top down communication	1 2 3 4 5	Open, relaxed two-way communication
7.	Unilateral decision-making	1 2 3 4 5	Collaborative decision-making
8.	Parental involvement controlled	1 2 3 4 5	Parents welcomed and integrated
9.	Limited investment in recruiting	1 2 3 4 5	Great care with selection procedures
10.	School environment not cared for	1 2 3 4 5	School environment shows pride and caring
11.	Curriculum planning reactive and pragmatic	1 2 3 4 5	Curriculum planning anticipatory and value-driven
12.	Budget planning reactive and incremental	1 2 3 4 5	Budget planning objective-driven
13.	Pastoral care marginal and a chore	1 2 3 4 5	Pastoral care implicit to all processes
14.	No monitoring or review	1 2 3 4 5	Constant data collection to improve processes
15.	We get by	1 2 3 4 5	We are going to be the best school of our type

Total score =

Results:
66–75 A total quality school.
56–65 The potential for quality.
36–55 The basis for change is available.
 0–35 There is a lot to be done.

Complete this review with regard to relationships between adults in the school and then with regard to relationships between adults and children.

Figure 6.2 School culture review

- What is the justification for perpetuating a hierarchical structure that diminishes personal responsibility?

One of the most significant features of total quality organisations is the abandonment of formal hierarchies and the reconstitution of the workforce in teams. The change from an almost Victorian stratification to teams constituted on the basis of being able to work effectively is one of the most powerful manifestations of cultural change.

As schools become increasingly autonomous in budgeting and staffing terms, so the opportunities are available to move from hierarchies to teams thereby giving tangible evidence of a belief in democratic processes and equality of opportunity. It never has been easy in schools to demonstrate a precise correlation between pay, status and function.

The implementation of a team approach also provides an opportunity to question the academic/pastoral divide found in many secondary schools. This again raises the issue of the way in which values and mission are put into practice and so create a culture. If the mission of the school is to 'educate the whole child' then it does seem inconsistent to have a structure which compartmentalises that educational process into discrete areas, thereby increasing the need for communication, liaison and specialist functions. Many special schools, in contrast, provide a model of an integrated approach to learning and social development.

The demands of the National Curriculum, records of achievement, cross-curricular initiatives and the increasing use of flexible learning all militate against traditional hierarchical compartmentalisation. The organisational practices of small primary schools and special schools may well provide a model: teachers having clearly designated responsibilities for functions over and above their classroom teaching and leading the rest of the staff, working as a team, when appropriate. It is becoming increasingly obvious in secondary schools that teachers may be involved in teaching two or even three subjects. As this trend grows the traditional structure will become increasingly irrelevant.

The total quality school's structure may be not a pyramid but rather a disc in which autonomous teams are able to interact with their customers, each other and with the centre. However, the centre only holds as much power as is necessary; authority and responsibility are delegated to teams commensurate with the tasks they have to do. The function of the centre is to provide leadership, to empower and to facilitate the teams.

Recruitment and selection

This topic has been chosen as an example because it exemplifies the changes that may be necessary to implement a quality culture. It is easy to caricature selection procedures for teaching posts in schools: application forms that have more space for O levels than for experience; advertisements that invite applications from 'dynamic, exciting and committed teachers looking for an opportunity to work in a challenging and rewarding school' with the candidate's being judged on the basis of a restricted application form and a twenty-minute interview.

Two factors have to be given equal weighting when approaching the selection process. First, the applicants are customers and are therefore entitled to a quality process. Second, the successful candidate has to be the one who cannot only do the job but who also shares the school's culture. The selection process has to be designed to maximise the chances of identifying the right person. Too often selection procedures are historic and confirm an individual's ability to do the present job, when they should be predictive. This implies clear specification of criteria for appointment, and the use of measurement, at the very least the collection of data, needs to be as objective as possible.

Techniques are available to support this approach.

- **Job specification:** this identifies the actual components of the job, what the duties will be and so specifies the knowledge, skills and experience necessary. It should therefore refer to age range, subject specialisation, ability range and management responsibilities. This is what the school wants the successful candidate to be able to do. The job specification is developed into an agreed job description only after appointment.

- **Person specification:** this is the sort of person the school wants and is the most problematic area but a crucial one if the individual is to fit into the team. A lot of work has to be done in identifying and defining the personal qualities appropriate to the post. Experience and knowledge are no guarantee of a social 'fit' and yet this is what will largely determine effectiveness.

- **Application forms:** these need to serve two purposes: to allow candidates the opportunity to describe themselves in a positive way; and to allow selectors to make a systematic comparison. Forms should be designed to facilitate these purposes. Letters and CVs are useful but make comparison problematic.

- **References:** these are useful if information specific to the post is sought, i.e. if the referee is asked to provide evidence or a judgement on the extent to which the candidate meets the person and job specifications.

- **Interviews:** the interview has significant potential as a selection process but equally has the greatest opportunities for abuse. In order to avoid sub-jectivity, bias and dissemination interviews need:

- agreed and understood criteria;
- consistent patterns of questioning for each candidate;
- an agreed means of recording data, e.g. a scoring matrix;
- trained interviewers;
- an appropriate setting with suitable facilities for the candidates.

- **Analogous testing:** even the most effective interview is limited in its ability to evaluate a candidate's ability to do the job. The use of activities which allow candidates to display skills and qualities appropriate to the post seems essential. In-tray exercises are a common form of this approach but a wide range of others is available. Most important, the capacity to teach or manage has to be reviewed; hearsay is not sufficient evidence.

- **Psychometric testing:** this remains a problematic issue but, if used in conjunction with a range of techniques, it has considerable potential to provide objective data to selectors. A wide range of tests is available covering skills and proficiency, aptitude and personality. The use of these tests is contentious, especially in an educational environment which most of them were not designed for. However, they can generate significant comparative data and provide the basis for more informed interviewing.

Accuracy of specification and carefully designed procedures related to the specification will produce data that will inform the final decision.

The selection process also needs to take into account the needs of unsuccessful candidates in providing feedback and advice. As much as anything else recruitment and selection are another component of marketing the school. In the context of reinforcing the culture of a school the selection process must at least minimise the chances of an inappropriate appointment. At best it will be a powerful manifestation of a quality culture.

Curriculum planning

The full implications of total quality for the curriculum are properly the subject of a separate study. However, in the context of school management there are some specific issues with regard to the management of the curriculum, largely concerned with reconciling customer needs with the deployment of teaching staff, time and resources. The central issue, especially for some secondary schools, is the extent to which the curriculum can be delivered and children's learning managed by one teacher in one classroom, teaching one subject for one period to one class. The concept of 'fitness for purpose' raises fundamental questions about the uniformity prescribed by the timetable. There is also the very real issue of trust and delegation. The increasing complexity of the curriculum may also be an imperative for change.

If a team-based approach to school structures is adopted then one of the most important elements to be delegated to the team is control of its time. This could imply a timetable that is primarily concerned with shared facilities, e.g. sports hall, science labs, or those in short supply, e.g. technology and music facilities. Otherwise the planning and balance of the delivery of the curriculum would be a matter for the team within the requirements of syllabuses and school procedures. This is an opportunity to reinforce a climate of trust, responsiveness and customer focus. It also empowers the team and helps to create autonomous work teams.

It would be for the team to determine the most appropriate deployment of teaching strategies but the notion of resource-based learning has the potential for greater customer satisfaction, since learning has the potential for greater customer satisfaction for children. There is also the significant potential for the creation of management and development time for teachers. This approach requires the implementation of resource-based learning, the negotiation of learning contracts and the development of skills in team work, time management and the acceptance of personal responsibility for work rate and completion tasks. The skills needed in adults to work in a total quality environment are replicated almost exactly in children. The prospects for shared learning and development are significant and exciting. Equally important, children will be developing the work skills appropriate to total quality environments in which they might seek employment but which are also relevant to further and higher education.

The creation of team bases also has the potential to enhance the environment and the increased opportunities for sharing between teachers can only enhance professional practice and improve the quality of life. Working with a group of disaffected fifteen year old pupils on a Friday afternoon, considering the economic consequences of World War II is an experience that needs to be shared with colleagues. There is nothing unique in this approach – it is already found in many primary and special schools and in the art and technology departments of secondary schools. What it does is to try to create a culture where the central purpose of a school – children's learning – can be managed in as consistent a manner as possible so that the culture is made tangible for adults and children and thereby reinforced.

These three examples have tried to demonstrate the relationship between culture, quality and the practical aspects of school management. However, it is important to stress that there can be no prescription. Schools need to understand for themselves the implications of quality approaches, identify the appropriate culture and ensure that management structures and processes are consistent with both.

Creating a total quality learning culture

Total quality is only a vehicle – it has no virtue or validity unless it is applied to a specific context. For it to work in schools it has to be given meaning through the identification of that which the various components of the total quality philosophy exist to do. The nature and purpose of education is a complex and problematic topic, since there is no consensus as to why schools actually exist – to teach the National Curriculum, to prepare young people for higher education and employment, to act as agents of social control, or indeed all of these. Multiplicity of purpose is one of the most inhibiting factors in introducing total quality into education. Given the momentum of social, economic and technological change it could be argued that the one common factor to these elements has to be learning – the creation of autonomous learners who can respond to change in a positive and life-enhancing way.

It might well be that the culture appropriate to a total quality school is that of a learning organisation. The issue is whether schools can become learning organisations using total quality approaches to help in the process.

Pinchot and Pinchot (1994) talk of the 'intelligent organisation' – not an unreasonable aspiration for schools perhaps. The culture of the intelligent organisation is captured thus:

> *Architectures of intelligent organisations will be flexible, shifting to meet new challenges and responding to local situations. What will make them responsive is not the brilliance of organisational designers sitting at the top but the decisions of people in the middle and bottom of the organisation who freely choose the connections needed to make their area work ... choice is widely distributed so that all members can contribute their diverse talents and experience and develop and express their intelligence. (p. 62)*

The culture of the intelligent organisation is one of trust, respect and recognition of the individual: a principle which would appear to be at the heart of most schools' aspirations for members of their communities. Although intention and moral conviction are almost always present in school aims and mission they are always invariably compromised by a mismatch between principle and practice.

Schools are committed to the notion of individualism and the freedom to learn but this, too, is compromised by inappropriate structures and systems which deny the intention in practice. A helpful notion here might be Gerard Manley Hopkins' notion of 'inscape' where there is harmony between the outward expression and the essence or unique inner quality of the object. Total quality provides the means to close the gap between intention and practice through changing the basis on which organisations are designed and managed.

107

However, changing structures and systems is not enough. In order to move a school into a total quality culture a number of fundamental principles have to be exemplified in organisation life.

The most important of these principles is learning. If it is the core purpose of a school then a number of fundamental implications follow.

- The school understands the social, psychological and, increasingly importantly, the neurological focus influencing learning.
- The relationship between learning and teaching and the role of the teacher is clear and consistently applied.
- The central characteristic of learning, that it is an individual and subjective process, is recognised in the organisation of the school.
- The management of the school is focused on managing the variables that influence the learning of individuals.
- Structures and systems are designed to facilitate learning and exemplify the principles of effective learning.
- Everybody in school is a learner; adults as well as pupils are experiencing the fun and joy of learning as well as the frustrations and fear of failure.
- Learning rather than teaching, knowledge, the curriculum etc. is the habitual mode of expression.

In essence the semantics and semiotics of the school together with its symbolism are all manifestations of an obsession with learning.

The other principles relevant to a school seeking to develop a total quality learning culture are derived from Pinchot and Pinchot (1994) and the critique of bureaucratic organisations. Seven essentials of organisational intelligence are argued for (pp. 61–74).

Widespread truth and rights

Freedom of enterprise

Liberated teams

Equality and diversity

Voluntary learning networks

Democratic self-rule

Limited corporate government

It is further contended that:

> These conditions are interdependent in the sense that they do not necessarily work well separately. They span the inherent paradox of human organisation – the advantages of high levels of freedom and rights, along with the benefits of strong community and sensible governance. Many of the best knowledge-based businesses are providing the conditions for lots of freedom and lots of interconnection. (pp. 63–4)

Application of the seven conditions to schools

Widespread truth and rights

Information is widely available making it possible for everyone to make better decisions and more informed contributions. There is open access to meetings and data. The total quality school is data-rich – information technology makes this possible and easy. The British obsession with secrecy (often extending to teachers' first names) is one of the major barriers to organisational growth and can only create an inhibited and closed culture – the antithesis of what is required for real learning. Such freedom of access has to be guaranteed. Schools could be said to need the equivalent of a Bill of Rights and a Freedom of Information Act.

Freedom of enterprise

This is especially pertinent to a school focused on learning.

> People need authority to make localised, decentralised choices in everyday work. In an intelligent organisation, everyone uses his or her individual intelligence to find problems to address, to decide whose help is needed, to do work in ways that make the most of everyone's talents, education and experience. In some sense virtually all knowledge work consists of making choices…
>
> Without freedom of action, individuals cannot use the full power of their intuition, their judgement or their experience. (Pinchot and Pinchot 1994, p. 66)

It is difficult to conceive of a more powerful manifesto for the creation of a culture based on learning.

Liberated teams

This issue is discussed in detail in Chapter 8 and it is not necessary to revisit the issue except to quote Pinchot and Pinchot:

> Teams serve as the autonomous unit of the system, as cells do in biological organisms and families do in free society. (p. 67)

Equality and diversity

The learning process has to reconcile the twin moral imperatives of ensuring quality and equity in all aspects of the organisation while respecting the integrity of individual diversity. A focus on the individual as learner increases the possibility of the harmonisation of these potentially conflicting demands. The more bureaucratic a system is, the more it is designed and managed around cohorts, the less likely it is to guarantee equity and to celebrate diversity.

Voluntary learning networks

Networking is the lifeblood of any organisation and is the natural corollary of Handy's Task Culture. The learning network is an ecological expression of the organisation, and is like a macrocosm of the way in which the brain functions along neural channels. An organisation which exemplifies fractal relationships of networks is demonstrating a culture focused on learning in which the core purpose is constantly reiterating through the experience of every individual. The more complex and sophisticated the social network the more likely it is to encourage the emergence of a learning-based culture.

Democratic self-rule

Pinchot and Pinchot argue very strongly (p. 72) that in the intelligent organisation democracy does not mean representative democracy. It must involve direct participation, control and decision-making. This is both a moral and practical imperative, that is, the school has to exemplify the principles of the society in which it is based. Equally, involvement through democratic action is one of the most powerful means of developing and maintaining commitment, motivation and involvement. Stakeholders have to feel they have control over that which affects them most directly and significantly.

Limited corporate government

This coincides closely with Handy's notions of subsidiarity and federalism (Handy, 1989, p. 100). The boundaries between governance at the centre and at the local level have to be carefully delineated to reconcile that which is necessarily corporate and that which is properly the domain of teams and individuals. The issue may be resolved in terms of using efficiency and effectiveness as criteria for making the judgement as to where authority and responsibility should reside. What is overwhelmingly important is avoiding the perpetuation of a dependency culture as this is alien to both quality and learning.

Summary

- An understanding of a school's culture is essential to quality management.
- Culture is the shared understanding of an organisation through rites, ceremonies, language and social interaction.
- There is a range of cultural models – none is right or wrong: the important thing is to understand which is yours.
- A quality culture has a number of specific and unique characteristics.
- Cultures are given expression through structure, focus, communications, style and responsiveness.
- The factors influencing culture are the practical issues of day-to-day management in schools.
- Learning has to be the key determinant of a school's culture.

Actions

1 Understanding your school's culture: is your perception shared by colleagues?
2 Is your school's culture given consistent expression through management structures and processes?
3 Do your management processes reflect learning processes and vice versa?
4 Review your own behaviour to establish how far it is consistent with leading and managing a quality culture.

7

■ ■ ■

Leadership

Introduction

Without appropriate leadership no quality programme will work; only dynamic leadership can create the commitment to drive the strategy. Equally leadership will serve as the most graphic example of what adopting a quality approach actually means in practice. The message is very clear – if there is not total involvement by leadership in quality, if it is not an obsession, forget it! It will not work and may well be counterproductive. The implication of this is that before the issue of quality is raised within the school the quality of leadership may need to be explored.

The purpose of this chapter is to explore the issue of leadership in the context of total quality by examining:

* traditional views of leadership in schools;
* the components of quality leadership.

Traditional views of leadership in schools

It is probably still valid to argue that the primary determinant in selection procedures in education is the capacity of the individual to do her or his existing job: the bulk of the selection process is based on historic data. When the process becomes predictive it is usually through interview questions, which may or may not be explored in depth and verified by the simplest of procedures. Questions on leadership will usually concentrate on the legal/administrative aspects of leadership: how to run a meeting, how to handle difficult parents, the LEA's administrative procedures etc. The issue is demonstrated in the research data produced by Hall, MacKay and Morgan (1986) and shown in Figure 7.1.

HEAD	TEACHING	ETHOS	POLICY	OPERATIONS/ ADMIN	HUMAN MANAGEMENT	EXTERNAL
A	14	12	0	25	36	1
B	41	4	3	32	8	12
C	31	12	0	18	27	12
D	0	20	26	10	20	7
E	34	19	1	18	17	1

Figure 7.1 Heads' time on task (percentage of time on main categories)

Although this is a limited sample covering a very limited time span it does indicate some highly significant patterns: for example, head B spends 73 per cent of her/his time on teaching and routine matters and only 15 per cent on what would generally be regarded as a leadership function, while head D by contrast spends 74 per cent of her/his time on what would be regarded as leadership activities.

Neither head is 'right' or 'wrong' in approach; the important thing is to reflect on the implications of the view of headship which avoids contact with people, as leader, and the implications for the school of limited attention to ethos, policy and personal relationships. It is the purpose of this chapter to argue that the approach to leadership exemplified by head B is inappropriate in the context of total quality management. The difference is between the head as 'doer' and the head as facilitator and enabler. It is equally important to raise the issue of the head's role as leader and her/his relationship with the senior management team.

1 How often do you sit and listen for the whole meeting?
2 Do you have a clear view of where the school will be in five years' time?
3 How often in the past year have you used the school's aims as the agenda for a meeting or training day?
4 How much time have you spent analysing and discussing your own development needs?
5 How much time do you spend checking the work of others?
6 When did you last listen to pupils talking about their experience of school?
7 How much of your time is spent 'firefighting'?
8 What proportion of your staff are ready for promotion?
9 What is the perception of your school in the community? How do you know?
10 Does your behaviour put into effect your principles of professional practice?
11 How much learning is going on in school? How do you know?

12 To what extent is your school a moral community?

13 How do you reconcile principle and pragmatism?

14 How much of your time is spent mentoring and coaching?

15 Do you make a difference?

If the answer to these questions are generally negative the reason advanced will probably be a lack of time. It might be a useful preliminary to implementing a quality programme to create 'quality time' and the first stage in this process is analysis (see Figure 7.2).

On the grid below enter what you believe should be your time allocation for each category. Select a 'typical' day and at five-minute intervals note down what you are doing. If possible get someone to track you for the day. Categorise each activity according to the following criteria:

Teaching and supervision: i.e. timetabled lesson or regular break or lunchtime duty.

Administration: low-grade, routine, clerical work not needing professional expertise.

Managing: routine meetings, organising, communicating, monitoring, interviewing, delegating, decision-making.

External relations: representing the school, dealing with the community.

Leading: planning, creating, empowering, being visible, driving the vision.

No contact: personal time spent not actually doing the job.

Calculate the percentage of time spend on each activity. Record the results:

	IDEAL ALLOCATION %	ACTUAL %	VARIATION
Teaching and supervision			
Administration			
Managing			
External relations			
Leading			
No contact			

Figure 7.2 Time use analysis

The analysis of your results is very much a subjective matter. However, if leading and external relations constitute less than 50 per cent of your actual time then it may be that there is a need for a significant review of your priorities and the way in which you organise your time. Quality management requires explicit leadership, not efficient administration, from the leading professionals. There are numerous self-help manuals available on time management and it is not intended to repeat the advice here. Rather it is argued that the components of effective leadership require detailed role analysis and clarification of expectations so that every individual has a range of responsibilities appropriate to her or his role.

The role of the deputy headteacher is a classic example of ambiguity that inhibits effective leadership. Very often responsibility is delegated but not authority, and this inevitably compromises the ability of individuals to act, requiring duplication of effort and so loss of time. Torrington, Weightman and Johns (1989) summarise this problem:

> *The work that deputies did varied enormously both within schools and between schools, but many were personal assistants to the headteacher rather than senior staff with clear and significant responsibilities justifying the status and salary. (p. 137)*

If quality management in schools is to work then it must be perceived as being the responsibility of the senior management team and not one individual – it is too large and complex a job for one person. Equally, the effective functioning of the senior management team sends one of the strongest messages about the nature of quality management. These issues are explored in more depth in Chapter 8.

One of the biggest problems in creating a total quality school in most English speaking education systems is the emphasis on the leadership and personal accountability of the headteacher. As has been shown there are significant problems in creating a shared concept of leadership within senior management teams. It is even more difficult to see leadership at work throughout the school. For a total quality approach to work leadership has to permeate every role in the school. This is best manifested through team structures but also needs to be encouraged in classrooms in the work of both teachers and students. Leadership has to be the 'warp' of the school, holding together every aspect of organisational life, not the embroidery applied for display.

Although schools need to be led by individuals (who do make a difference) that overarching leadership has to be replicated right through the organisation and found in every aspect of school life. A useful metaphor here is the notion of fractal leadership: it shouldn't matter how much the school is magnified the same essential pattern of leadership will be found.

The components of leadership that are described in the following section are as relevant to teams, classrooms and student groups as they are key to the work of the headteacher or principal.

The effective team or classroom requires vision as much as the school. The behaviours of effective leaders are as necessary for curriculum and pastoral leaders as for senior staff. As Murphy (1997) expresses it :

In the community of leaders, the school moves from achievement to transformation. Eventually, all are involved in the vision, all play an active part in transforming the organisation, not simply managing it… as the community of leaders matures, more and more become involved in the school, the governors, the parents and most important of all the students. (p. 137)

Fundamental to any discussion of leadership, however widely distributed, is clarity as to the essential purpose of that leadership. For Hill (1996) there is no doubt that student learning and achievement has to be at the heart of leadership activity and that:

the main impediments are of an organisational and systematic nature and concern the understandings, commitment and resources needed to transform ordinary schools into high performance adaptive learning organisations characterised by purpose, coherence, internal alignment and effectiveness. Overcoming such impediments calls for effective leaders who make as their first priority the improvement of classroom teaching and learning. (p. 11)

The components of quality leadership

The literature on total quality and excellence is quite explicit about the components of leadership. Although there are semantic differences, two issues emerge as being most significant: first, the importance of distinguishing between leadership and management, and second, specifying the appropriate behaviour for leaders.

Much has been written about the relationship between managing and leading. For some writers leadership is a sub-set of management; for others leadership is too intangible a concept to be discussed usefully and the emphasis is therefore on operational issues. This leads to the situation described by Hall, MacKay and Morgan earlier in this chapter. HMI has consistently argued that leadership is one of the crucial determinants of an effective school. Schools that are perceived as being less than effective are probably being managed, more or less successfully, rather than being led.

The key differences between leading and managing are demonstrated in Figure 7.3.

This is not to diminish the significance of managing; it is a crucial determinant of organisational success but it has to operate within a context and according to

LEADING is concerned with:	MANAGING is concerned with:
VISION	IMPLEMENTATION
STRATEGIC ISSUES	OPERATIONAL ISSUES
TRANSFORMATION	TRANSACTION
ENDS	MEANS
PEOPLE	SYSTEMS
DOING THE RIGHT THINGS	DOING THINGS RIGHT

Figure 7.3 Leading and managing

explicit criteria and it is the function of leadership to provide that context and those criteria. Senior management teams thus need to be concerned with values, direction, the long term and, crucially, enabling others to fulfil the central purpose of the school.

In order to achieve this, it is proposed, there are four key components to leadership in a quality environment:

- vision;
- creativity;
- sensitivity;
- subsidiarity.

These components are not offered as a hierarchy; indeed they are highly interdependent and each presupposes the others to be fully effective. If these components are found either in individuals or distributed in teams then the context for managing will be created. Most importantly the school will develop the capacity to become a learning or intelligent organisation that is capable of changing through the process of continuous improvement.

The management of change has been regarded for some time as a central component of leadership. The changes in educational policy over the past ten years have required schools to respond to multiple, externally imposed innovations. The result has been to reify change – to give it a significance as another component of effectiveness rather than as a fundamental manifestation of organisational life. The danger of 'managing change' is that it implies that there will be periods when it will not be necessary to change – change becomes a topic or product rather than the central abiding process. It is virtually impossible to create a culture of continuous improvement if change is seen as a distinct entity to be managed.

Vision

Much that has been discussed in Chapter 5 applies to this section. The emphasis here, however, is on the shared vision of headteacher and school leadership. Somewhere in the job description of headteacher and senior staff, and in the published functions of leaders, there needs to be a reference to the responsibility for generating and driving the school's vision. This will involve consultation and communication but it should be seen as a fundamental task without which all other activity will be at best reactive, at worst peripheral and random.

The purpose of vision is to help the school move from the known to the unknown; to set out the hopes and aspirations of the school for children, community and staff. Crucially the vision articulates and defines the values of the school, making them real and attainable. The vision has to be expressed in images, metaphors and models so as to organise meaning for all those involved in working in the school. The well articulated vision helps to answer the questions 'Why are we doing this?', 'What should we be doing?' and 'How should we be doing it?' etc.

The clarity and practicality of a school leadership team's vision will do much to determine the success or failure of a school. The decisions relating to pupils' learning, community involvement, decision-making and the development of teachers will have a significant impact on the standing of the school in the community.

The school leadership team that has a clear vision is characterised by:

- clarity of moral purpose;
- constant reference to the vision in action;
- frequent recognition of future challenges;
- constant contact with all members of the school community;
- openness to ideas;
- recognition and celebration of strengths and successes.

The senior management team that lacks vision will be primarily concerned with:

- routine decision-making and problem-solving;
- bureaucratic relationships;
- 'distant' personal relationships;
- constant stress on failure and weakness;
- reinforcing the status quo.

A vision needs to reconcile a wide range of factors in order to provide the basis for empowering leadership.

118

1 It needs to focus the moral and aesthetic dimensions of work; it must give expression to what is perceived as good and beautiful – the ideal that is aspired to. Education lends itself to the expression of such values as few other social activities do.

2 The vision must be challenging and inspiring and act as a focus for motivation; it must articulate an ideal which challenges the mundane and rejects conservation of the norm simply because it is the norm.

3 The vision must reinforce success and celebrate strengths – paradoxically it must consolidate that which is valid and be capable of responding to a changing environment at the same time.

4 The vision should talk in terms of ideals and principles and yet be capable of being translated into specific action. Above all the vision must be capable of being communicated, and of becoming meaningful to everyone to whom it applies. This means children, parents, non-teaching staff, governors and the wider community as well as teachers. It should be possible to identify concrete steps towards attaining the vision.

The process of actually articulating the vision requires high-level reflection and introspection – the outcome of this meditation needs to be shared, tested and refined and, crucially, responses listened to. The questions asked in Figure 7.4 might help clarify the issues.

---

1 If my child were a pupil at this school, what would I expect for her/him?

2 What are the major externally imposed challenges that we will have to meet?

3 What do our clients really want?

4 What are our most significant skills and capabilities?

5 In what ways are we unique?

6 What is our potential as a school?

7 What are our most significant successes?

8 What problems do we need to overcome?

9 What can we learn from other schools?

10 How will we know that we are getting it right?

11 Looking back over the past five years, what would I change?

12 What single thing must we get right?

Figure 7.4 Evolving the vision

As has been argued in Chapter 5 vision is the result of three elements:

- core purpose;
- morality;
- futures thinking.

The relationship between individual and collective vision is complex and problematic. It does seem to be the case that the most successful schools (and organisations in general) have a high degree of commonality in these fundamental issues. At the same time educationalists have traditionally sought a high degree of personal autonomy. This can be a highly creative tension but it can also be dysfunctional and potentially destructive.

The answer would appear to lie in Senge's (1990) view of alignment which he describes as:

> commonality of purpose, a shared vision, and understanding of how to complement one another's efforts. Individuals do not sacrifice their personal interests to the larger team vision; rather the shared vision becomes an extension of their personal visions. (pp. 234-5)

Covey (1989) makes a similar point:

> synergy works; it's a correct principle… it is effectiveness in an interdependent reality – it is teamwork, teambuilding, the development of unity and creativity with other human beings. (p. 283)

Leadership cannot be discovered from team working yet in many ways leadership is team working. The notion of the individualistic leader is as redundant as that of the charismatic leader. A practical example of shared vision is found in the National Commission on Education (1996) report on Lochgelly North Special School:

> In terms of a sense of shared values it is exceptional. To describe shared values as tangible may seem extravagant, but from the moment of entry to the school the visitor cannot but be aware of a community of purpose. It is positive and optimistic, expressed in smiles, in touch and gesture…
> It comes from talking and planning, challenging and learning from one another. (pp. 122–3)

Creativity

It is frequently stated that education reforms have challenged all existing assumptions about the management of schools. If this is the case, and there is little reason to doubt it, then reliance on traditional approaches to management are inappropriate. Indeed, the use of traditional techniques and solutions may be counterproductive if not actually detrimental. One of the principal factors in headteachers taking early retirement has been a natural reluctance to abandon established methods of working. However, unique problems require unique solutions. Creativity, the generation of imaginative and radical solutions to apparently intractable problems, thus becomes an essential component of leadership.

It is again important to stress that this function, although a highly desirable individual trait, is substantially enhanced through a team approach. No amount of dedicated reading of management 'self-improvement' manuals will bring about flashes of creativity: working in teams can release creative power. These issues will be explored in more depth in Chapter 8. It is worth reiterating that the sum of the parts is greater than the whole and that it has been consistently demonstrated that teams are more creative, more likely to generate radical alternatives and are better placed to review and evaluate possible solutions. At the same time individuals do need to generate solutions and creative thinking is a skill that can be developed.

Characteristics of the creative thinker
1 Being at ease with complexity.
2 Being relaxed with abstract concepts.
3 Using a variety of problem-solving approaches.
4 Synthesising rather than describing data.
5 Persisting with an apparently intractable issue.
6 Not being afraid of being wrong.
7 Displaying naïveté in questioning.
8 Accepting all possible solutions, no matter how apparently ridiculous.
9 Accepting possible solutions from any source.
10 Visualising all possible viewpoints.
11 Organising data in a variety of permutations.
12 Being aware of a range of sources for solutions through reading and networking.

Many of these characteristics are to be found in the notion of 'helicoptering': the ability of an individual to rise above the minutiae of a situation, to place it in context, identify the best solution and then descend with a clear view of what needs to happen. Flying the helicopter helps to identify the wood and the trees, to note the paths and the clearings and to avoid blundering around in circles in the undergrowth convinced that working hard is a substitute for solving the problem. Some problem-solving techniques are identified in Chapter 10 but they are largely for use in groups; the following are suggested individual strategies.

Self-analysis

What kind of thinker are you? What are your values? What are your 'hidden agendas'? The answers to these questions form a fundamental precursor to developing creative approaches. A person's intellectual history, e.g. their academic training, may well determine the extent to which they are conservationist or creative. The level of personal security will influence the level of change that can be tolerated, the openness to new ideas. The process of self-analysis may lead to the decision to make better use of the skills of colleagues, to change working practices or to seek training.

Targeting

This technique involves selecting a very specific issue or process and generating as many new ways of approaching it as possible. The topic might be very mundane, e.g. litter in school, or very complex, e.g. improving communication with parents. The technique is to write down a new way of approaching it which describes what will actually happen, i.e. the strategy must be expressed in terms of action. This technique works best if 'anything goes' – all ideas are worth considering.

Challenging

This approach involves questioning the status quo, asking 'What if?' questions, reflecting on what would happen if established roles and procedures were broken, generating alternatives to the established work patterns: 'Why does X always do this? What will happen if it is not done? What will happen if somebody else does it?'

Thinking skills

Creativity and generating ideas are skills that need developing like any others. The works of Edward De Bono and Tony Buzan may be worth exploring to this end.

Transferring

This process involves speculating on alternative scenarios and may involve reflection on how other cultures, institutions and historical or contemporary figures might respond to the situation. This approach can also be parasitic: taking an idea from a course or conference or reading and speculating on its applicability. Creativity often consists of reordering or rearranging existing ideas to suit a particular situation.

Quality thinking

This is the most complex and intangible approach and could be described as reflection or even meditation. The process has five components.

- **Recognising** the years of experience, understanding and intuition and letting them become a resource.
- **Synthesising** that experience by a process of reflection and ordering.
- **Explaining** all the facets of understanding by focusing very precisely on all the constituents of an issue.
- **Drawing** on the intuition to enhance appreciation and awareness.
- **Formulating** responses based on the improved awareness.

This activity may be significantly improved by training in meditation techniques or it may be thirty minutes in the day for undisturbed thinking. In schools there is a desperate need for leaders to have thinking time. It is usually lost, swamped by day-to-day demands. These demands are real and important but the issue is: 'What are the implications of leaders not thinking'?

Fundamental to all these points is the notion of leader as learner. This is intrinsically important for three reasons:

1 The leader (of school, team or classroom) is seen as a model or exemplar of good personal and professional practice.
2 Leaders should understand what it means to be a learner, the joys, the tears, hopes and anxieties of learning.
3 Leaders can improve their capability through habitual learning.

The leader as learner is someone who:

- is critically reflective of her/his practice;
- seeks regular feedback;
- monitors and reviews her/his performance;
- identifies new skills and knowledge to be acquired;
- exposes him/herself to new situations;
- works with a learning network;
- has a mentor/coach;
- experiences failure;
- listens to others;
- understands how others learn.

Sensitivity

There are three concerns in the area of interpersonal skills for leadership: first, the quality of personal relationships will often be a prime determinant of client satisfaction; second, there is a need for consistency in all processes; and third, the behaviour of leaders is a crucial model in the implementation of a quality programme. In schools, where social relationships are the fundamental and most significant process, it is difficult to overemphasise the centrality of high-level personal skills. The behaviour of leaders will be a key determinant in motivation, in creating a culture and forming the reactions of those with whom leaders come into contact.

For these reasons sensitivity has been chosen as a key characteristic – sensitivity in relationships with others but also sensitivity in personal aware-ness of the impact made on others. The major problem is that personality cannot be legislated for: no series of prescriptions will change inappropriate behaviour (possibly quite the reverse) so self-awareness is a crucial component of developing sensitivity. There are many courses offered in the area of interpersonal skills so it is not appropriate to offer diagnostic activities in the context of this book. Instead an inventory of relevant skills and behaviour is proposed that suggests the following characteristics are particularly relevant:

- listening;
- giving feedback;
- negotiating;
- giving praise;
- managing conflict;
- networking;
- empathising.

Isolating these characteristics in this way might create a false impression, because they are highly interdependent and each presupposes the others if sensitivity is to be practised successfully. The desired outcome is best exemplified in the notion of 'win–win'. This describes one of the four possible outcomes from any transaction, a situation summarised in Figure 7.5.

We win	I win you lose
I lose you win	We lose

Figure 7.5 Winning and losing

There is clearly one desirable outcome – that we both win. All other variants imply defeat for one or both parties and this can only serve to diminish both, to exacerbate personal relationships and compromise self-esteem. Win–win does not imply compromise or dilution but rather sophisticated skills which build on a foundation of respect. Win–win situations are most likely to result when:

- all desired outcomes are expressed;
- commonality is sought and emphasised;
- the emphasis is on the problem, not the person;
- alternative solutions are proposed;
- the emphasis is further on process and outcome;
- the implications of both losing are recognised.

In order to achieve the situation of 'us' rather than 'me' the skills identified as follows are all relevant and have to be incorporated into the criteria for appropriate behaviour.

Listening

Most people can hear perfectly adequately but only a minority can actually listen in the sense of genuinely attending. Active listening, i.e. total involvement, is difficult but vitally important as it demonstrates commitment and involvement and ensures that information is gathered and correctly received. Listening is as much about the unspoken as the spoken, it is about sensitivity to feelings and perceptions. Active listening requires:

- eye contact at regular intervals;
- body language which is supportive and reinforcing, e.g. attentive body posture, nods and smiles, reinforcing hand gestures and positive sounds;
- providing regular feedback;
- using reinforcing questioning styles to corroborate and confirm;
- avoiding negative behaviour, e.g. being distracted, fidgeting or allowing interruptions.

Giving feedback

Giving feedback is a demanding but highly significant skill, it involves reiterating to the speaker what she/he has just said. It checks the accuracy of listening, allows confirmation of feelings and reinforces the significance attached to what has been articulated. In essence the listener 'plays back' what has been said but also checks interpretation. Feedback works best when:

- it is non-judgemental;
- it uses the same language;
- feelings and perceptions are confirmed;
- the information given is built on;
- it is specific to the individual;
- agreed criteria are employed.

However, feedback serves another fundamentally important function in that it demonstrates the respect, seriousness and commitment of the listener.

Negotiating

Negotiating skills are concerned with reaching an outcome, taking a decision, solving a problem and, at the same time, improving personal relationships and enhancing mutual esteem. In order for this to happen a number of very specific skills and behaviours are necessary.

- Focus on the issue not the person.
- Build on proposals 'yes, and. . .' not 'yes, but. . .'.
- Obtain and agree facts.
- Explain and justify differences.
- Articulate feelings.
- Use the full range of questioning styles.
- Summarise and feedback.
- Generate mutually agreed alternatives.

Giving praise

This is one of the most neglected areas of leadership in schools. Teachers who are consistent in their belief in the importance of praising children consistently fail one another. Praise implies recognition, celebration and reinforcement: fundamental needs of adults as well as children. However, there is a need to avoid gratuitous and superficial responses. Genuine praise consists of many characteristics:

- It is specific to an individual.
- It refers to a specific event.
- It gives reasons.
- It is unconditional.
- It is not linked to an ulterior motive.
- It is given at the time, on the spot.

Managing conflict

Conflict in organisations is almost inevitable and, if properly managed, it can be a powerful stimulus to action, creativity and the resolution of hidden tensions. Managing conflict means that that conflict is not avoided or 'glossed over', but rather dealt with directly and explicitly. Positive conflict management involves:

- openly recognising that there is a conflict;
- understanding the motives at work;
- depersonalising the issues;

- empathising with the other person;
- avoiding prescriptive statements;
- generating alternative solutions;
- continuous feedback to confirm understanding;
- accepting incremental solutions;
- agreeing monitoring procedures to ensure implementation.

Networking

Networking is the process of establishing and maintaining a series of co-operative relationships that help get things done. Successful leaders have the ability to identify those who can help, i.e. people with the knowledge, access or skills, and the ability to mobilise that help. Active networking involves nurturing contacts, reciprocating support and identifying those who need to be cultivated. The most important indicators of an effective network are:

- effectiveness of communications;
- importance attached to regular contact;
- time for regular contact;
- offers of reciprocal support;
- use of the network to facilitate specific agendas;
- clear identification of who can help to get things done.

Empathising

This is the ability to understand how things seem to another person, to appreciate the significance, value and relevance attached to a given situation. Any form of communication is likely to be compromised unless there is a willingness to accept that subjectivity defines reality. Obtaining real understanding involves:

- active listening;
- checking through feedback;
- understanding 'why' as well as 'what';
- demonstrating recognition of the situation;
- challenging to clarify;
- talking about one's own experience;
- visualising the situation.

Sensitivity is thus about caring, respecting and cherishing. It only has meaning when it is expressed in action and this implies:

- creating winning situations;
- listening first;

- understanding;
- collaborative problem-solving;
- emphasising process issues;
- awareness of others.

Subsidiarity

By general consensus headship has become an almost impossible job; the demands are so great and the imperatives often so contradictory that many find it physically and psychologically overwhelming. One of the factors involved is the burden of expectation on headteachers, especially in primary schools. The traditional response to this has been the advocacy of empower-ment and delegation, and these are discussed below according to the conventional models. However, before discussing these concepts it is worth raising the issue of subsidiarity – a fundamental challenge to the concepts of empowerment and delegation. According to Handy (1989), the principle of subsidiarity as derived from the doctrines of the Roman Catholic Church:

> holds that 'it is an injustice, a grave evil and a disturbance of right order for a large and higher organisation to arrogate to itself functions which can be performed efficiently by smaller and lower bodies.' To steal people's decisions is wrong. (p. 100)

He further argues that it means giving away power.

Empowerment and delegation are manifestations of a control and dependency culture. 'I empower you.' 'I delegate to you.' In other words I am dispensing power and, by the same token, I can take it away again. You only have as much authority as I choose to give you and it remains at my behest.

This is bizarre in organisations where the core purpose is the creation of autonomous learners. Subsidiarity is best manifested through the concept of the autonomous or self-managing team where the team has responsibility and authority, control over resources and the ability to make real decisions without reference. The greatest inhibitor of delegation and empowerment is having to seek permission. A fundamental corollary of subsidiarity is first letting go, leaving alone and being concerned only with the achievement of agreed outcomes, not with the means. This applies as much to the individual learner as to the team.

Subsidiarity in practice would involve what Handy calls a federal structure, something that the British psyche with its centrist tendencies finds very difficult to come to terms with. Given the skill and ability of teachers and managers in education there is no reason why they should not be trusted in the same way as workers in many businesses are.

However, the transition from control to trust and from delegation to subsidiarity requires a fundamental reorientation which might take some time. Genuine delegation is a significant transitional phase to the sort of structure described in Chapter 8.

Schools are contradictory institutions when it comes to delegation. On the one hand they delegate awesome levels of responsibility and authority, for instance to the classroom teacher who has a high degree of personal autonomy, but on the other they are unable to replicate this when it comes to management. The failure to delegate inevitably implies a limitation on involvement and thereby a lack of trust.

Real delegation has a number of significant benefits.

- It is a real and direct demonstration of trust; it translates the rhetoric of trust into a tangible expression.
- It is one of the most powerful means of facilitating development allowing real learning to take place by doing the job.
- It forces a radical evaluation of the key purpose of a job and questions those aspects which may be enjoyable or therapeutic but are still best delegated.
- It creates the time to lead by delegating management and administrative tasks more appropriately done by somebody else.

Delegation is a balancing act between a number of variables: accountability, control, authority, responsibility and training. Accountability cannot be delegated as that would amount to abdication, which is totally inappropriate. Therefore a measure of control has to be retained. However, control can be maintained through setting and reviewing targets as much as by constant reporting and checking. Delegation without authority is unfair and unworkable and is not true delegation as it implies constant referring back, which defeats the object of the exercise. If authority is delegated then so must be responsibility, as a degree of personal autonomy is then established. Responsibility without authority is cruel and a recipe for failure. If both are effectively delegated then ownership is created; the job becomes a real one rather than the 'dumping of chores'.

Leaders or managers who state that they are unable to delegate because 'the staff aren't up to it' or 'they are bound to mess it up' are condemning themselves rather than the staff. If staff have not been trained and developed that is the responsibility of the manager, not of the employees. As part of the delegation process, training needs have to be identified at the outset in order to ensure that motivation is matched by capability. The components of delegation are shown in Figure 7.6.

Unless there is full autonomy in all components of the job, delegation will not work. The delegator will not have 'let go' and the delegatee will not feel fully

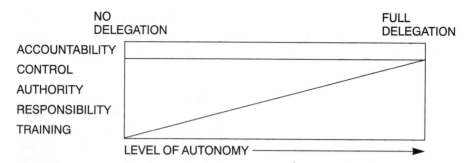

Figure 7.6 The delegation process

trusted. If the other components of quality management are in place then delegation is not only 'no risk' but is actually seen as a normal way of working. As with so many aspects of total quality, models already exist in some schools, in the effective classroom, for example.

- The underlying purpose is clear, understood and accepted.
- Clear targets are negotiated and agreed.
- The timescale is established.
- Criteria for acceptable performance are clear.
- Outcomes and check points are defined.

If these structural issues are clear then the next stage is for the delegator to adopt appropriate behaviour.

- The delegatee initiates contacts, not the delegator.
- Responsibility is publicly located with the delegatee, and this is reflected in private. There is constant reinforcement.
- Requests for information and decisions are referred to the delegatee.
- Questions are met with questions, not prescriptions.
- Requests for resources are met on merit, not seen as signs of failure.

Delegation empowers because it has the potential to demonstrate trust, create real, purposeful jobs and, crucially, it provides a vehicle for self-actualisation, esteem and achievement. Managing children's learning is all about these factors. It is ironic that what happens in the classroom is not always mirrored in the staffroom.

In order to make delegation work the following stages might be followed.

1 Is your job description up to date and accurate? Does it reflect the key purpose of your job?
2 Does the reality of your working life reflect your job purpose? (Use the time use analysis in Figure 7.2.)

3 On the basis of this analysis identify those parts of your job:
- which only you have the skills, knowledge and experience for;
- which are unique to your seniority and responsibility;
- which are routine and standardised;
- which consume a disproportionate part of your time;
- which do not require your skills, knowledge and experience.

4 Which members of your staff are ready for promotion, development, in need of change, ready for redeployment?

5 Use the appraisal process to identify and reconcile school needs, individual needs, opportunities for development.

6 Identify training needs, train and let go.

In essence empowerment is about seeing people as being capable of infinite improvement and development. Organisations exist to enhance people, not to stultify them. Every leader has to recognise that each single employee is a customer, entitled to quality in all aspects of their lives.

Leadership and quality

Total quality is fundamentally about improvement; leadership in the quality organisation has to be about transformation leadership and change and transformation have to be synonymous – no leader has ever been regarded as successful because of an ability to sustain the status quo. The most effective leaders are people who are involved in personal change so as to facilitate organisational growth. Figure 7.7 sets out the components of leadership for changing organisations.

Leadership is a complex phenomenon. It is much easier to be normative than descriptive and it is difficult to find a definitive model. It may well be that leadership has to be seen as a heuristic process full of contradictions. Gardner (1995) identifies a number of issues and paradoxes in the debate about leadership:

- the tension between technical expertise and the need for shared under-standing;
- the need for stories that reach many individuals;
- the potential of such stories to broaden or fragment a sense of community;
- the balance between the distribution of knowledge across a group and the ease of dealing with one leader;
- the knowledge that leaders are limited in what they can accomplish;
- the issues of manipulation, influence and co-operation;
- the need to aid leaders;

KNOWLEDGE	SKILLS	BEHAVIOUR
INDIVIDUAL MOTIVATION	LISTENING EMPATHISING	CONSTANT REFERENCE TO THE VISION VALUES PEOPLE – AND SHOWS IT
ORGANISATIONS AS SOCIAL SYSTEMS	GIVING FEEDBACK QUESTIONING	BREAKS BUREAUCRACY REINFORCEMENT OF SUCCESS
THE SCHOOL'S ENVIRONMENT	TARGET SETTING	WORKS ON FACTS LEADS BY EXAMPLE
MANAGEMENT PROCESSES	CONFLICT MANAGEMENT MANAGING LEARNING	OBSESSED WITH CUSTOMER SATISFACTION
CHANGE PROCESSES	ANALYSING SYNTHESISING	TOLERANCE OF AMBIGUITY
LEARNING STYLES	CREATIVITY	OPTIMISTIC OUTLOOK
CUSTOMER REQUIREMENTS	PROBLEM-SOLVING	ACCEPTANCE OF FAILURE
DEVELOPMENT STRATEGIES	COUNSELLING DELEGATING COMMUNICATING	LOW ESTEEM NEEDS CELEBRATION OF WORK AS FUN ALWAYS AVAILABLE OPENNESS PROVIDES A MODEL

Figure 7.7 The components of leadership for managing change
(*Source*: derived from Everard and Morris 1990 and Peters 1988)

- the choice between direct and indirect leadership;
- the tension between rational and spiritual dimensions. (p. 305)

These tensions and concerns do not diminish the possibility of leadership; rather they point to the centrality of the need to see leadership as a process, as a series of decisions and relationships which create meaning in a given context.

One of the most potent images of the 20th century is that of the wagon train in the Hollywood Western. The wagons progress serenely across the prairie following the trail blazed by the leader (who is usually motionless on a hilltop highlighted by a convenient sunset). She has delegated responsibility to outriders who manage the actual progress of the wagons, work out the precise route, mend broken wheels and circle the wagons when danger threatens. At the back of the wagon train is the chuck wagon (crewed by an irascible old man and a youth with an unfortunate tendency to break into song). The wagon train will quickly fall apart, lose its way and its purpose if the leader spends her time in the wagon counting the beans, worrying about the bacon and measuring out the coffee. She brings about improvement by being in front. Leadership is about the sunset, not the beans.

Summary

- Traditional approaches to headship may not be appropriate in the context of TQM.
- Leading and managing need to be carefully distinguished.
- Self-analysis is an essential prerequisite of effective leadership.
- Leadership is not the monopoly of the head.
- Vision is the driving force for leadership.
- Creative problem-solving is an essential characteristic.
- Sensitivity in terms of personal relationships is a fundamental requirement.
- Leadership is about empowering others.
- Leadership is about changing.

Action

1 Find out how your leadership style is regarded by your colleagues.
2 Use the appraisal process to review your personal effectiveness.
3 Analyse your use of time – how much leadership time are you losing by doing the mundane and routine (however satisfying)?
4 Are the deputies in your school leaders or clerks?
5 Identify a leader whom you admire, spend time shadowing her/him and set up a mentoring arrangement.
6 Invest in two days' team thinking time (a weekend in a good hotel can cost less than a day's supply). Use a consultant to facilitate the process.
7 Use the appraisal process to empower your colleagues.
8 Explore the opportunities for leadership and team development training.
9 In the next senior appointment you are involved in, identify detailed criteria for leadership characteristics and the means to assess them.

8

■ ■ ■

Teams

Introduction

A team is a quality group. Almost all organisations, and schools in particular, create teams as the major vehicle for organising work. However, there is a substantial gap between labelling a group a team and creating an effective work team which is able to function in a total quality environment. Too often teams are established and expected to operate simply by virtue of having delegated tasks – little consideration is given to the way in which the team actually functions. Designing and developing teams is rarely seen as a priority in schools. They are created by virtue of knowledge, experience and status, not by the ability of the individuals to work collaboratively. The purpose of this chapter is to examine:

- the significance of teams;
- the characteristics of effective teams;
- team building;
- team development;
- quality circles;
- developing team-based schools.

The significance of teams

Effective teams have come to be seen as one of the crucial characteristics of quality organisations and, equally significantly, one of the most powerful catalysts in an organisation for implementing change. As Katzenbach and Smith (1993) explain:

> *In any situation requiring the real time combination of multiple skills, experiences and judgements, a team inevitably gets better results than a collection of*

134

individuals. . . teams are more flexible. . . teams are more productive than groups. . . .
Teams and performance are an unbeatable combination. (p. 15)

However much emphasis on team work has become commonplace of management writing schools do seem to be remarkably unwilling or unable to convert themselves into team-based organisations. This may be attributed to three related factors. First, the organisational structures and career patterns of education are profoundly hierarchical. Second, the concept of professional autonomy has led to, and consistently reinforces the notion of individual working and personal accountability. Third, the actual organisation of many schools means that teachers are geographically isolated for much of their working day. (What percentage of your week is spent working away from other adults?) This culture of individualism is at the heart of many of the dysfunctional aspects of school life and even when teachers do come together *unaligned* their capacity to work as a team, rather than as a group, is inevitably *team* constrained. Senge (1990) describes this phenomenon as the 'unaligned team' with individuals with varying levels of power heading in different directions:

The fundamental characteristic of the relatively unaligned team is wasted energy.
Individuals may work extraordinarily hard, but their efforts do not efficiently
translate to team effort. By contrast when a team becomes more aligned, a
commonality of direction emerges, and individuals' energies harmonise. There is less
wasted energy. (p. 234)

Senge contrasts the coherent and focused light of a laser with the diffuse and incoherent light of a light bulb in which a substantial proportion of the energy is dissipated as heat, or hot air – a well known phenomenon in ineffective groups.

A further significant attribute of a team-based approach is related to organisational growth and development. Organisations cannot learn, only individuals can, and they then articulate and share their learning in order to create a common understanding. In most circumstances we learn better in teams. Taylor and McKenzie (1997) demonstrate how an approach to team learning for students has had an impact on teachers' behaviour.

Teacher collegiality is increased; they discuss problems that arise, deal with issues
that are of importance to them and provide support for each other. This model steps
beyond the token gesture at collegiality, largely anecdotal, to be a more sophisticated
and useful form of professionals treating each other with respect and developing
meaningful, practical solutions to the challenges that are faced by the team. (p. 153)

More importantly perhaps is the fact that the way teachers work together is a model for the way students work together:

These students have the opportunity to experience success, through working co-operatively and sharing their unique knowledge with others in a structured situation. Co-operative social behaviour is taught and developed.... They also understand that a team approach to problem-solving or assignment work is often more welcome.... as there is a richness in the quality and quantity of ideas. (p. 154)

Much of our learning takes place through articulation, explanation, questioning, modelling and responding to others. These processes are much more likely to be effective if they take place in a socially sophisticated environment, i.e. a team. Simple sociometrics will indicate that we are unable to relate effectively with all the members of the organisation to which we belong. An optimum number appears to be between four and twelve, depending on the task. Organisations therefore need to be seen as the sum of their teams, just as teams are the sum of their members, but with the potential to be greater than the sum. Organisational learning and thus growth and improvement are only likely if individuals are learning in aligned teams.

A final manifestation of the significance of teams is to be found in what might be termed personal integrity and potential. Although many of the greatest breakthroughs in art and science are highly and uniquely personal most of us live in response to others, we create meaning and develop social understanding through our patterns of social relationships. Teams, therefore, may be a highly significant component in personal realisation. Covey (1989) argues this point as follows:

The person who is truly effective has the humility and reverence to recognise his own perceptual limitations and to appreciate the rich resources available through interactions with the hearts and minds of other human beings. That person values the differences because those differences add to his knowledge, to his understanding of reality. When we're left to our own experiences, we constantly suffer from a shortage of data. (p. 277)

Teams do make a difference – there are abundant analogies to be drawn from sporting activities but they can all be summarised by considering the relationship between sporting expertise and skill, leadership and team success. Technical skill does not guarantee success, the expert practitioner is not necessarily the best captain, and assembling the most talented individuals does not always create a winning team. Just as expertise with the cricket bat is not necessarily indicative of leadership skills, so expertise in the classroom is no guarantee of the ability to collaborate with colleagues. There can be a real tension between the autonomy (and isolation) of the classroom and the need to work in a team. This view is reflected in the work of Murgatroyd (1985) and Torrington, Weightman and Johns (1989); synthesising their views produces an analysis of the problematic nature of teams in schools.

1 School 'teams' place great emphasis on the tasks (agendas) of managing and little emphasis on the processes (networks). 'Getting the job done' is seen as more significant than how the job is done. However, the lack of concern with process can often be to the detriment of task achievement.

2 'Teams' in schools lack a 'bias for action' – they spend too much time debating issues and principles (over which they may have little or no control) and too little time solving problems, formulating solutions and developing a commitment to action. Groups debate – teams act.

3 Poorly managed 'teams' in schools are reactive – responding to events rather than anticipating them and often seeking solace in routine chores rather than driving the vision and becoming anticipatory. This leads to work becoming a chore and ritualistic.

4 'Teams' are often not concerned with their own social needs. They spend insufficient time recognising, reinforcing and celebrating each other. Equally they will not devote time to planning and reviewing their work nor will they seek to develop their skills as a team or the potential of individuals to become effective team members.

The working of these 'immature' teams will often be characterised by very formal social exchanges (e.g. the use of titles rather than first names); the use of quasi-parliamentary procedures (e.g. 'On a point of information, headmistress, may I enquire through the chair. . .?); the reading of documents to the team and the active pursuit of red herrings (e.g. debating the influence of social hierarchies of 19th-century England when planning the seating arrangement for prize giving).

At best teams are a compromise between individual perceptions, needs and values and organisational imperatives. The tension between the individual and the organisation can never be truly reconciled but teams offer the best hope of respecting individual integrity and the demands of the organisation. More positively teams offer the basis for enhancing the individual while allowing the school to function.

The characteristics of effective teams

A synthesis of the research of McGregor (1960), Likert (1961) and Blake and Mouton (1964) produces the 'map' of effective team functioning, shown in Figure 8.1.

The strength and creative potential of teams is derived from the application of each of these characteristics, but more importantly from the critical mass achieved when they are linked and synergy is achieved. At that point the 'whole' is considerably greater than the sum of the parts. Each characteristic is

137

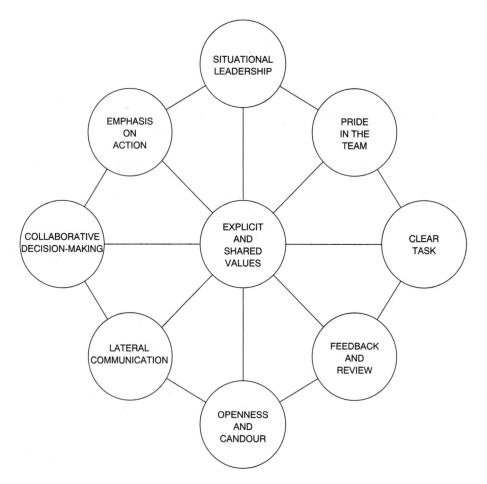

Figure 8.1 The components of effective team work

complex and demanding in its own right and needs to be explored in some detail.

Explicit and shared values

This issue has already been explored in Chapters 5 and 7. However, it is worth stressing that no team can operate effectively unless it is working in a context where the values are clear and agreed and translated into a mission. Equally it is important that the personal values of team members are public and understood. Each person knows the values everyone else brings to the team so they are not being continually debated (see 'forming' and 'storming' in Figure 8.4).

Situational leadership

The principles discussed in Chapter 7 are particularly relevant here. Effective teams require leadership that displays all the characteristics explored previously. However, in the context of team working a new dimension is necessary: the willingness and ability of the designated leader to defer, to stand back and allow other team members to assume control according to the needs of the situation. This implies a detailed understanding of the knowledge and capabilities of each team member and the 'grace' to pass on authority. For example, a deputy headteacher may have highly sophisticated decision-making and interpersonal skills and so is the best person to chair management meetings. A relatively junior member of staff may be the most knowledgeable about flexible learning – she should be allowed to lead and is entitled to the wholehearted support of the team. In this way the team is effective and a team member is empowered.

Pride in the team

This implies commitment and involvement and is manifested in high morale and loyalty. Team members believe in themselves, in each other and in the team as a whole and this is expressed frequently both internally and externally. There is a self-fulfilling belief: 'We are good and we can deliver quality'. Departments in schools that are doing well and feel good about themselves quickly transmit this. There is even the possibility of displays of enthusiasm.

Clear task

Without a clear task effective team work is impossible. Teams that are set intangible goals, unclear outcomes and lack information, resources and a timescale are unlikely to be motivated; in fact they are more likely to plod and amble rather than sprint. For a team to sprint it requires:

- specific outcomes;
- performance indicators;
- realistic targets;
- information and resources;
- nurture and reinforcment;
- a timescale.

Sprint teams have their eyes clearly on the tape, know exactly how far they have to travel and explode into action. Too often in schools teams are sent on country rambles when they need to be racing. To alter the sporting metaphor somewhat, teams do not win by debating if the goal posts are moving – they win by scoring goals.

Feedback and review   *The learning element*

Effective teams are very self-conscious; they devote time to getting feedback from their clients and from each other. Team review is a permanent feature of every activity. This is not introspection for its own sake but rather review as part of a learning process. The review of task completion and team processes provides the basis for change through learning. Sophisticated teams will abandon the task to explore what is happening in process teams – to identify and reinforce success and to tackle problems until they are solved. The team that does not invest in itself is unlikely to add value to its way of working (see Chapter 9 for review techniques).

Openness and candour

All issues are open to discussion, there are no 'hidden agendas' and every member of the team feels able to offer suggestions, ideas, comments, information, praise and criticism. Relationships are comfortable and relaxed and the climate is supportive; 'Yes, and...' is used rather than 'Yes, but...'. Criticism is frank and direct and aimed at the problem not the person. Further, it is not negative but is used to remove an obstacle. Team members express their feelings as well as their opinions on the task; the effective team cultivates the ability to talk easily about emotional and personal responses.

Lateral communication

Effective teams are also characterised by lateral communication; team members are able to communicate with each other without reference to the team leader or other members of the team. Complex networks are formed and nourished by the team – they are not seen as a threat but rather as potential enrichment. Equally, sub-sets within the team are open and report back. This process in itself develops skills and reinforces relationships to the benefit of the team as a whole.

Collaborative decision-making

Effective teams make the best decisions – the decision is the 'best fit' and will be fully implemented by team members. Quality decisions emerge from the full utilisation of the knowledge and skills of the team members, which means that the decision will have been made in the minimum time but to maximum effect. Collaborative decision-making avoids voting, alternative viewpoints are worked through and disagreements resolved. Crucially the team is enhanced socially by the decision-making process.

Emphasis on action

Teams make things happen – their decisions are expressed in terms of action. Each team member knows what has to be done, by whom and when. Effective teams do not write minutes of their meetings – they issue agreed actions.

Effective teams expect to accomplish the impossible. Miracles may take a little longer. Teams balance task and process – what the job is and how it is done (see Figure 8.2). Position A represents an ideal, the optimum to be worked for where the task is achieved effectively and there are high-level personal relationships. Quality is delivered in terms of product and process. Any other position on the grid compromises one or both. High concern for tasks with little regard for process denies the social significance of work; high concern for process at the expense of task removes the point of the team's existence. The design, recruitment and development of the team will have a significant impact on its outcomes both in terms of task and process.

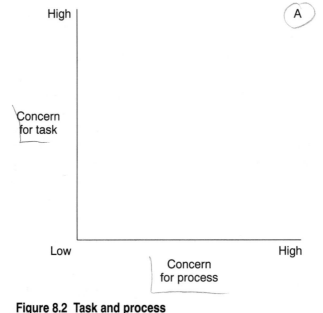

Figure 8.2 Task and process
(Source: after Blake and Mouton 1978)

Team building

Effective teams do not happen by chance; they have to be created deliberately and managed systematically. Given the significance of the outcomes of educational decision-making and the pressures on the time of teachers and managers in schools the importance of creating effective teams cannot be overstated. Teams in schools are rarely created with principles of team building in mind. Team membership is often a low-order selection factor if it is an issue at all. Induction is likely to be in terms of administrative procedures if it takes place.

It may be appropriate to distinguish between structural and ad hoc teams in schools. Structural teams will include the senior management team, academic and pastoral units and groups set up to manage specific issues such as the curriculum, budget or staff development. Ad hoc groups are set up to manage specific issues, e.g. cross-curricular initiatives, implementation of a particular reform or event. In both cases the capability of teachers to work as leader or member of a team will not be an issue. Membership will be on the basis of experience, status or volunteering. Significance might be attached to consultation; rarely will the capabilities of the person as a team member be a factor. This might help to explain the frustration often experienced by so-called team members in schools – the frustration arises because they cannot function as members of teams. Figure 8.3 provides a starting-point for analysing team effectiveness.

Complete this analysis thinking of a team of which you are currently a member. Score each section according to how you perceive the applicability of each set of statements.

1. Values and purpose are not discussed	1 2 3 4 5	We share and implement common values
2. Leadership is restricted to one or two people	1 2 3 4 5	Leadership is shared according to need
3. Team membership is a chore and a bore	1 2 3 4 5	There is genuine pride in team membership
4. Objectives are not shared or understood	1 2 3 4 5	We are committed to our objectives
5. We never talk about how we are doing	1 2 3 4 5	We systematically review our performance
6. Communication is restricted, cautious	1 2 3 4 5	Communication is open, robust, honest
7. The team leader dominates	1 2 3 4 5	Our abilities are fully utilised, we are trusted
8. Decisions are taken by voting or by the leader	1 2 3 4 5	We all share and support decisions
9. Action is unclear or absent	1 2 3 4 5	We all know who does what by when

Figure 8.3 Team effectiveness analysis

A score in excess of 35 indicates that the rest of this chapter is probably redundant; 25–35 indicates there will probably be something of interest to you; 9–24 I just hope this chapter can meet your needs. Once you have completed this analysis get other members of your team to complete it independently. Then use a team meeting to discuss your perceptions by displaying the scores on a flip chart or OHP and analysing the significance of any discrepancies in perceptions. If your score is below 20–25 it will probably be very difficult to get this review on the agenda.

Another means of analysing the maturity of the team is to consider its level of development. Tuckman (1985) suggests that teams go through a series of clear stages in the move to effectiveness, as illustrated in Figure 8.4.

TASK	STAGE	PROCESS
CLARIFICATION OF OUTCOMES SOUGHT, ROLES UNCERTAIN	FORMING	ANXIETY, UNCERTAINTY, DOMINATION, AMBIGUITY
VALUE AND FEASIBILITY OF TASK QUESTIONED, PRINCIPLES AND METHODS DEBATED	STORMING	CONFLICT BETWEEN GROUP'S RESISTANCE TO LEADER, INDIVIDUAL INITIATIVES, OPINIONS POLARISED
PLANNING STARTS, WORKING STANDARDS LAID DOWN, ROLES CLEAR	NORMING	WORKING PROCEDURES ESTABLISHED, COMMUNICATION OF FEELINGS, MUTUAL SUPPORT, SENSE OF TEAM IDENTITY
SOLUTIONS TO PROBLEMS EMERGE, MORE OUTPUT IN LESS TIME, QUALITY OF OUTCOMES IMPROVES, DECISIONS ARE TRANSLATED INTO ACTION	PERFORMING	HIGH LEVELS OF TRUST AND INTERDEPENDENCE, ROLES ARE FLEXIBLE, INDIVIDUALS AND TEAM RELAXED AND CONFIDENT

Figure 8.4 Stages in team maturity

The central principle in team building is to minimise the time spent forming and storming, to make norming as powerful as possible and to devote the maximum amount of time to performing. It is not possible to 'short circuit' the process, i.e. avoid forming and storming, but with deliberate team management the negative aspects can be minimised. Analysis of the way in which some teams work suggests that they never get beyond the first two stages, all their time being spent in debating the task and sorting out personal relationships. Eventually they have to accept an imposed decision and are unable to produce acceptable conclusions in the time available. There are a number of possible explanations for this.

p. 129

1 The task itself is impossible – it has not been properly defined or is beyond the resources of the team, i.e. it is inappropriate.

T/Design

2 The team has not been designed to accomplish the task, i.e. the wrong people have been nominated or allowed to volunteer.

T/Devt

3 The team lacks the skills to work together.

p. 129

The first problem can be resolved only by appropriate delegation (see Chapter 7); the second issue is dealt with below and the third in the next section of this chapter, team development.

If teams are to move rapidly from forming to performing then the capabilities of team members to work in a team have to play an important role in team design and recruitment. Some of the most important work in this respect has been done by Belbin (1981). Belbin analysed the performance of management teams and found that there was not always a correlation between a team's ability to perform and the intellectual qualities and experience of its members. In fact, the so-called 'alpha' teams – the brightest and best – were often out-performed by apparently random groupings. In analysing the reasons for this Belbin concluded that the behaviour of individuals in teams may be more significant a factor than either ability or experience. Teams are social entities and their performance will be determined by social interactions and these, according to Belbin, can be identified and analysed.

Belbin (1993) postulates nine team roles as outlined in Figure 8.5.

Team Design

Belbin's team roles

A person's team characteristics are identified on the basis of completing a diagnostic inventory. This will usually identify one or two roles that score significantly higher than others, i.e. the dominant types of behaviour. Other types will receive very low scores and are probably not available. The interpretation of individual results needs to bear a number of points in mind:

- there are no 'right or wrong' or 'good or bad' types – all are valid and appropriate;
- the balance of the scoring will probably indicate a range of possible team behaviours;
- the scoring will reflect the types in a given context at a certain time – both factors are variable and scoring can change;
- the secondary type can often be developed.

Role	Contribution	Allowable weakness
Plant	Creative, imaginative, unorthodox Solves difficult problems	Ignores details Too preoccupied to communicate effectively
Resource investigator	Extrovert, enthusiastic, communicative Explores opportunities Develops contacts	Over-optimistic Loses interest once initial enthusiasm has passed
Co-ordinator	Mature, confident, a good chairperson Clarifies goals, promotes decision-making, delegates well	Can be seen as manipulative Delegates personal work
Shaper	Challenging, dynamic, thrives on pressure Has the drive and courage to overcome obstacles	Can provoke others Hurts people's feelings
Monitor/ evaluator	Sober, strategic and discerning Sees all options Judges accurately	Lacks drive and ability to inspire others Overly critical
Teamworker	Co-operative, mild, perceptive and diplomatic Listens, builds, averts friction, calms the waters	Indecisive in crunch situations Can be easily influenced
Implementer	Disciplined, reliable, conservative and efficient Turns ideas into practical actions	Somewhat inflexible Slow to respond to new possibilities
Completer	Painstaking, conscientious, anxious Searches out errors and omissions Delivers on time	Inclined to worry unduly Reluctant to delegate Can be a nitpicker
Specialist	Single-minded, self-starting, dedicated Provides knowledge and skills in rare supply	Contributes on only a narrow front Dwells on technicalities Overlooks the 'big picture'

Figure 8.5 Belbin's team roles

Although the Belbin inventory provides the basis for useful personal insights and self-appraisal it is even more powerful if used by a whole team as the basis for analysis of the team's working patterns. This can be a useful exercise at the forming stage. Consider a team that is made up of three shapers, one chair and a company worker. It is more than likely that the storming stage will reach hurricane proportions as the majority of the team will be striving to be dominant and the company worker will have a negative experience. If status is added into the equation then the chances are that the team's inability to function will lead to decisions being made outside the team and imposed.

The converse example is also problematic – a team that is composed of company and team workers with perhaps a resource investigator is just as likely to fail to achieve its task. A further issue for schools is that, on the basis of observation, many teams in schools lack monitor evaluators and completer finishers. This has significant implications for teams being able to complete tasks on time and according to specification.

The effective team, the quality team, is one that balances team roles so that task completion and the process issues are balanced. There can be no prescription for the ideal or optimum team but there do seem to be some guidelines:

- there should be one chair or one shaper, not both;
- according to the size of the team there should be a balance of team and company workers;
- other types should be included according to the nature of the task.

The senior management team of a highly regarded secondary school has the following make-up:

Post	Primary role	Secondary role
Head	Resource investigator	Chair
Deputy (Curriculum)	Implementer	Shaper
Deputy (Pastoral)	Chair	Team worker
Senior teacher (Admin)	Completer	Implementer
Senior teacher (TVEI)	Team worker	Resource investigator

More by luck than planning the school is led by a team that has a range of complementary roles with secondary roles that allow for flexibility according to circumstances. Research in one primary school revealed that the head was a shaper/team worker and all her staff were company/team workers. Harmony reigned but the burden on the head was enormous. A working party on appraisal in one particular secondary school failed perhaps because the designated chair was a company worker, the other members of the group were either shapers or innovators and there was no completer or monitor evaluator.

Belbin's work is problematic – the inventory was not designed for use in the education sector, his types derive from a study of small groups on management courses and the scientific validity of his research has yet to be fully tested. However, his work has met with a high degree of acceptance and it does provide the starting-point for detailed and systematic analysis. In the context of team building the Belbin inventory can help by:

- providing data for the analysis of team working and so facilitating discussion;
- indicating possible causes of failure and potential remedies;
- acting as a dispassionate means of discussing individual behaviour;
- identifying the composition of a team and so informing team development needs;
- helping with recruitment of team members when other appropriate factors have been taken into account;
- diagnosing individual development needs;
- identifying factors in team success, so allowing them to be replicated.

Team building is too complex to be left to serendipity. There are undoubtedly many already successful teams – but perhaps they could be better. Time is too precious to accept unsatisfactory teams as inevitable, team membership being a crucial determinant of an individual's perception of work.

Belbin demonstrates that teams that are successful:

develop well informed self-insight and took appropriate action in managing their style of operation. (p. 50)

Such action:

needed to be triggered off by an awareness of the collective self-image and a desire to manage what was there effectively. A coherent self-image emerged therefore, not only as an advantage for the progression of individuals, but for the team itself. (ibid.)

Team development

Effective teams result from empowered individuals learning to collaborate so that individual knowledge, skills and qualities are deployed to maximum effect. The group is one of the most powerful learning vehicles so the effective team has the potential to heighten the learning of its members if its standard operating procedures are perceived as learning opportunities. This involves an understanding of:

- how teams learn;
- what they need to learn;
- what techniques are appropriate.

Teams learn by relating experience to analysis and by changing their behaviour in the future (see Figure 8.6).

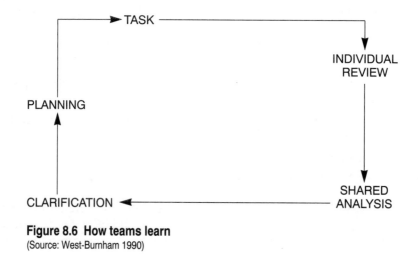

Figure 8.6 How teams learn
(Source: West-Burnham 1990)

Having completed a task individual members of the team review their own behaviour, that of their colleagues and of the team as a whole, both in terms of task achievement and team processes. These individual perceptions are then shared and a consensus view of the team's performance emerges: problems are identified, reasons for failure established and the factors involved in success celebrated and reinforced. This allows the team to clarify, to understand its behaviour and so agree how to approach the next task, what behaviour to stress and what to minimise so as to improve its performance. Three vital functions are taking place in this process.

1 The team is learning from direct, real experience – the most powerful learning agent.
2 The team is looking to improve its performance continuously.
3 The learning process is part of the work process – there is no artificial divide in terms of significance or loss of work time.

Two changes in team management are necessary to create a learning team. First, time has to be built into the team's activities to allow for planning and review; in essence this means that review becomes an agenda item. Second, this review needs to be detailed and systematic ensuring that every team member feels able to contribute fully. This implies a range of skills that need to be developed.

The components of effective teams identified in Figure 8.1 provide the context from which team training needs can be identified. In many ways the list corresponds to any portfolio of management development activities. The crucial difference is that the training is for the team as an entity and not in piecemeal form for the individuals in it. Too many team development courses are attended by individuals representing the team – this inevitably compromises the impact and integrity of the training. The team that trains together develops together.

The skills appropriate to effective team working are set out in Figure 8.7. This list might appear somewhat intimidating unless it is recognised that:

- teams will not work effectively without them ('If you think training's expensive, try ignorance');
- they are generic skills and will transfer into a wide variety of situations, notably the classroom.

LISTENING	COLLABORATING DECISION-MAKING
QUESTIONING	PROBLEM-SOLVING
GIVING FEEDBACK	CONFLICT RESOLUTION
SUMMARISING	TIME MANAGEMENT
PROPOSING IDEAS	STRESS MANAGEMENT
BUILDING ON SUGGESTIONS	MANAGING MEETINGS
BEING OPEN ABOUT FEELINGS	PUBLIC SPEAKING
ASSERTIVENESS	WRITTEN COMMUNICATION

Figure 8.7 Skills for effective team work

The methods that are appropriate to the development of these skills are widely understood but not always applied.

1 The team must train and learn together.
2 It is often easier to start the process away from the work place.
3 Consultants/facilitators can drive the process and help keep the focus.

4 Non-threatening activities, the notorious management games, are often the best way to start.

5 Outdoor team development can be very powerful, instructive and fun.

6 The training should be designed by team members on the basis of perceived need.

7 The training should focus on the issues of implementation.

8 The initial event should be seen as the start of the learning process, not the process itself.

9 Team activities subsequent to the training should make constant reference to the lessons learnt.

10 The skills and expertise of team members must be used as a permanent resource.

Team training and development activities are rather like circling the earth in a space shuttle. The angle of reentry is crucial – too steep (or enthusiastic) and the team is burnt up in the rich atmosphere of colleagues' cynicism; too shallow and the team bounces off the atmosphere, doomed to circle the real world and become management consultants. Training works if it is manifested in behaviour – there is no other justification for it.

Quality circles

The quality circle movement is one of the most frequently cited manifestations of total quality management. It emerged in Japan in the early 1960s and has been used across the world as a major strategy to involve 'shop floor' and production workers in a drive for quality. The primary motivations behind the movement have been to create a sense of involvement and ownership and to strengthen the feeling of workers as craftspeople. An immediate question has to be raised about the applicability of such a technique to professionals who are working in teams, however immature those teams might be.

The key characteristics of quality circles are:

- 3–12 members;
- people doing the same job or process;
- attendance is voluntary;
- regular meetings, perhaps one hour per week;
- meetings take place in working time;
- they are led by the 'supervisor';
- they identify, analyse and propose solutions to work-based problems;

- they recommend solutions to management;
- they implement those solutions.

The crucial thing about quality circles is that they are trained in the use of analytical problem-solving methods so that those with responsibility for making a process work are directly involved in the improvement of that process – their experience is respected and their solutions implemented. The quality circle movement has probably had as many failures as successes, the latter being mainly due to a lack of commitment, inadequate training and a lack of seriousness on the part of management.

There is little doubt that quality circles provide a useful model, most importantly in the transfer of responsibility to those who actually have to do the work. Their voluntary nature is clearly problematic and it would be nonsense to diffuse limited time and energy by having teams and quality circles in parallel. There may well be a case for arguing that the approach is valid for non-teaching staff given their different contracts of employment; however, this implies an unacceptable hierarchy of quality which would clearly be inappropriate and counterproductive. The answer would seem to be to combine the principles of effective quality circles to create what Peters (1988) calls 'self-managing teams'. In essence self-managing teams have a high degree of autonomy – everyone is a member of a team of between eight and fifteen people, teams assume direct responsibility for much of their workload and there is very limited specialisation within teams. Individual appraisal and pay are limited to the team's work.

The detailed implications of this approach are discussed in Chapter 6 but it is worth restating the issue of hierarchy, the role of middle management in a team environment and the importance of consistency in a total quality environment.

Developing team-based schools

Very little attention appears to have been paid to the principles influencing the design of schools as organisations. It is difficult to find theoretical or practical justifications and legitimations for the way in which schools are structured, organised and how the staff in them are deployed in terms of roles and responsibilities. A casual review of the basis on which many secondary and large primary schools are designed might draw the following conclusions.

- The structure is fundamentally hierarchical.
- There are high levels of specialisation.
- Many tasks are individual.

- Communication and co-ordination are significant problems.
- Bureaucratic procedures dominate many processes.

What emerges from this limited analysis is a Taylorian organisation concerned with administrative efficiency. Of course, schools are not like this in reality. They are highly complex places attempting to reconcile a vast range of individual needs within an organisational setting constrained by time and limited and diminishing resources. Yet if we look at the actual experience of individuals in schools it is often represented in terms of generic and mechanistic systems.

Inductive analysis of the experience of the individual within the school would point to conformity, power-based relationships and 'being processed'. If learning is taken as the core purpose of a school as a social institution then the individual's experience is often generic, artificially constrained by time and based on cohort progression which may bear no relationship to actual learning needs. The use of the class and year-based timetable delivered through subject compartmentalisation may be efficient but its effectiveness may have to be called into question.

A central principle of organisational design is that 'form should follow function', i.e. the notion of organisational ergonomics, creating the best possible fit. A maxim of engineering design is that 'if it looks right, it probably is right', but to what extent do schools 'look right', or in quality terms are they 'fit for purpose'? It could be argued that there is a major conceptual gap, a real lack of synergy between what schools exist to do and how they are structured to do it. It would be appropriate to argue that many small primary schools and special schools do not share this problem simply by virtue of their size, but hierarchy and bureaucracy can and do exist in any social institution. Mohrman *et al.* (1995) provide a useful analysis of what they identify as routine and non-routine:

Routine work	Non-routine work
Programmed	Emergent
Repeated patterns	Varied, unique
Analysable	Interdependent
Well understood	Uncertain
Static	Dynamic

On the basis of this analysis it might be possible to argue that the delivery of the curriculum is routine work and thus amenable to a formal structure. However, learning is surely non-routine. Mohrman and her colleagues argue that most 'knowledge work' is non-routine and therefore requires a new type of structure – the team-based organisation.

Organisational designs that were suitable for routine work in stable environments no longer fit most organisational settings. Increasingly, organisational success depends on making complex trade-offs, learning and implementing new approaches, and applying advanced knowledge. (p. 11)

It is easy to argue for team-based organisational structure in functional terms. Two other factors need to be taken into account when considering the design of schools. The first is a moral argument: the way in which schools are organised should be a practical exemplification of the principles they espouse as their core values. If these are based on notions of democracy, the significance of the individual, trust and the importance of collaborative and interdependent working then it is difficult to see how a bureaucratic hierarchy can be justified.

Second, Sawatzki (1997) notes that a central imperative in all organisations is enhancement of staff performance. It was noted in Chapter 1 that the context in which schools are operating is changing rapidly and one of the key imperatives is the need to enhance individual and so organisational performance.

In the high performance era, the team, and not the individual becomes the major unit of analysis. . . .
It should come as little surprise that such an arrangement is currently enjoying increasingly high levels of support from organisations of all kinds. This is because it is a manifestation of the belief that in high-performing, responsive, customer-focused organisations which are striving for success in this era, power, information and resources need to be allocated as close as possible to the point of delivery of services. (p. 150)

The case for a team-based structure appears overwhelming, but unfortunately in education we have comparatively few examples of schools fundamentally realigning themselves. One of the attractions of a hierarchic, bureaucratic control culture is that it does make life simple. However, in so doing it creates a dependency culture which must be anathema to those concerned with the full realisation of human potential through learning. In the final analysis it may well be that the major incentive to move away from hierarchy is an expedient one – management structures are expensive and the cost of management may well be the biggest single item of expenditure in a school's budget after staffing itself.

Figure 8.8 is an attempt to represent, in an abstract manner, the possible structure of a team-based school. A number of points need to be made about the model.

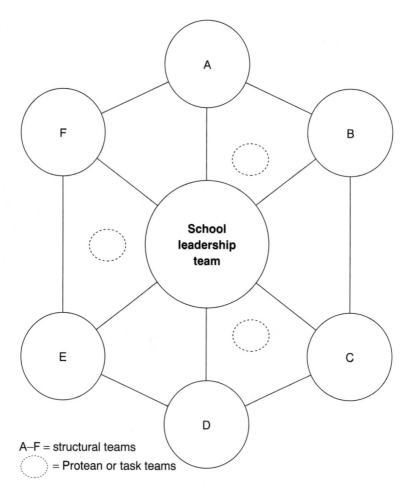

Figure 8.8 A team-based structure for a school

1 The school is a flatarchy, made up of a principal, team leaders and team members.

2 The school leadership team (think of the semantics of senior management team) comprises the principal and the team leaders although others can be involved as necessary.

3 The school leadership team is responsible for leadership, i.e. mission, strategy and development. The structural teams, working as self-managing, autonomous teams, are responsible for a specific cohort of adults and students.

4 Each structural team is in turn comprised of teams which are focused largely on the learning of students. These learning teams are led by the students themselves.

5   Protean and task teams can be created across the structural teams for a wide variety of activities, e.g. subject liaison, sporting events, cultural and social activities etc.

Aspects of this model already exist in many primary school classrooms. Indeed the classroom that is focused on the learning of the individual pupil (as opposed to the activities of the teacher) represents a microcosm of the school organised on quality principles. For many schools the issue is to extrapolate the good practice found in the leadership and management of learning into the leadership and management of the whole school.

Teams will never work properly, nor realise their full potential if they are grafted onto an existing hierarchical structure. Teams are probably the one form of organisational structure that comes closest to what is meant by the learning organisation. Of course there are still many uncertainties about the implementation of a team-based approach but as Mohrman *et al.* expressed it:

> *These changing organisations provide exhilarating opportunities for the development of new knowledge. The development of sound organisational practices and systems depends upon replacing the old bureaucratic paradigm with a new one. That paradigm is being developed as more is learned about this dynamic organisational form. (p. 367)*

Summary

- A team is a quality group and quality programmes depend on effective team work.
- Teams in schools are often teams in name only.
- Effective teams display nine key characteristics.
- Clear values, pride and appropriate leadership are requisites to effective team working.
- Teams cannot operate without a clear task, regular feedback and review, and openness and candour.
- Team processes involve lateral communication, collaborative decision-making and outcomes in terms of action.
- Effective teams balance task and process.
- Team building requires awareness of the stages of team development and the factors influencing individual behaviour.
- Team development involves seeing learning as a crucial component of team activity.
- Teamwork requires a range of generic skills.

- Quality circles are not an alternative to teams but do provide an alternative perspective.
- Effective teams may well mature into self-managing teams with significant implications for roles and school structures.

Action

1   Review any team of which you are a member in terms of:
    - its ability to get things done;
    - its social maturity;
    - its use of training and development.

2   For any team for which you are leader:
    - plan the introduction of review sessions;
    - analyse the extent to which you have empowered team members;
    - review your own team role.

3   Look at the way in which teams work outside school. What can you learn from them?

4   Agree a plan of action to make your team a quality team.

5   Reflect on the extent to which your organisational structure is 'fit for purpose'.

9
■ ■ ■

Managing Processes

Introduction

One of the great clichés of the quality movement is the notion of working smarter not harder. This is usually seen as being achieved through the adoption of a range of techniques which facilitate team working by structuring analytical and decision-making processes. The techniques are deceptively simple but provide a clarity and structure to collaborative working, a focus on core purpose and all enhance working relationships as well as reducing the waste of time usually experienced in meetings – a classic example of waste.

A variety of techniques are described which are designed to help measure and structure techniques to improve work processes. Some are quantitative, others are structured in such a way as to facilitate analysis of complex situations. None of these techniques is new to schools; all have been used before, if not always in the manner described. In the context of quality management they are not so much techniques to be employed as ways of working. It is important to place them in the context of effective team functioning, to see them as skills and tools which facilitate a team approach. All of these approaches require practice and review in order to work effectively.

The techniques described are:

- benchmarking;
- brainstorming;
- cause and effect diagram;
- five 'hows', five 'whys';
- forcefield analysis;
- measurement charts;
- Pareto analysis;
- problem-solving techniques;

- readiness and capability;
- statistical methods.

Benchmarking

This is one of the most widely used techniques in total quality organisations and is essentially an exercise in comparative analysis. In the commercial sector it is examining a competitor's product to establish in what ways it is better, or worse, to test the quality and examine customer satisfaction.

Benchmarking already takes place in education: it is one of the principal reasons for attending courses and conferences and reading the educational press. In essence it is about finding good ideas and ways to improve existing practice. However, it may be more appropriate to adapt a more systematic and detailed approach. This process works best with a specialist team although it may well draw on the experience and expertise of a range of teams.

Aim

To improve on best practice.

Step 1 Review

- Identify the process or product to be improved.
- Identify those who 'do it better'.
- Gather hard data to inform analysis.

Step 2 Analysis

- What factors contribute to their success?
- Is their product/approach right for us?
- What are the implications of adopting their approach?

Step 3 Planning

- What can we achieve?
- How are we going to achieve these outcomes?

Step 4 Action

- Implement specific actions.
- Monitor progress against norms.
- Go back to the original and review.
- Consider ways of extending improvement.

This process can be carried out on the basis of good practice in different schools. However, it is likely to be more effective within a school. What happens in other teams, departments and classrooms is likely to be a powerful source of improvement. Internal benchmarking has the additional advantage of helping and supporting review and development processes.

Brainstorming

This is a technique used to generate the maximum number of insights and involve all members of the work team on equal terms. It is particularly powerful in generating solutions to apparently intractable problems and in situations where creativity is at a premium. Brainstorming optimises the range of possible solutions and produces lists of ideas that can be evaluated, prioritised and rank ordered. The technique can be used several times in succession, e.g. (1) problem identification, (2) solution generation, (3) implementation strategy.

Brainstorming works best in groups of 5–10. The process should be managed by a facilitator (not necessarily the team leader) and each session should last from 10-20 minutes.

Step 1

- The problem or issue being reviewed is written on a flip chart or blackboard.
- Each member of the team suggests ideas which are written up without alteration or comment.
- The facilitator encourages each member of the team to contribute as many ideas as possible.
- The following 'rules' are applied at this stage:
  - No criticisms or judgements.
  - No evaluation.
  - No discussion.
  - No problem-solving.
  - Anything goes! All ideas are valid.
  - Everybody is asked for more ideas.

Step 2

The facilitator takes each suggestion in turn and checks with all members of the team to ensure understanding and accuracy of recording.

Step 3

The ideas generated are reviewed for duplication, trivia, the impracticable and inappropriate. Team consensus is needed before any factor is abandoned.

The ideas that are left are now subject to evaluation by applying criteria to them. Criteria might include cost (e.g. a specified limit), staff availability, training required, feasibility, consistency with agreed strategies. Again the team's view on the 'best fit' should prevail.

Step 4

The outcomes that meet all criteria are potential solutions which may be self-selecting or require further discussion in order to produce a rank order.

Cause and effect diagram

This technique is also known as fishboning or an Ishikawa diagram after the Japanese management writer who developed it (see Figure 9.1). It is one of the

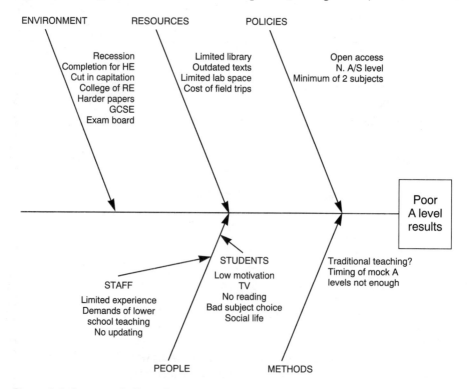

Figure 9.1 Cause and effect diagram

most widely used techniques in quality circles and one of the most powerful diagnostic and team development activities. In some respects it resembles brainstorming but is more structured and focused.

The process can be used to identify the causes of a problem by structuring and displaying them in relation to each other, and to analyse a process by reviewing factors which may be problematic. The systematic application of a cause and effect diagram can:

- identify all the causes of a problem;
- distinguish causes from symptoms;
- analyse the relative significance of related causes;
- provide data for use with other techniques.

The cause and effect approach works best with an established work team led by a facilitator. A maximum of one hour should be spent on process.

Step 1

Display the diagram (Figure 9.1) on a flip chart, OHP transparency or black/whiteboard. State the problem briefly at the 'head' of the fish. Decide what the characteristics of the 'ribs' should be. It may be helpful to select the most relevant from this list:

- method, procedures and stages in the process;
- materials, resources used directly or indirectly;
- people, skills and knowledge;
- measurement, the availability of appropriate data;
- environment, factors influencing the process;
- policies, the principles informing the process.

Step 2

Using brainstorming techniques generate the causes of the problem, placing each on the appropriate rib.

Step 3

The facilitator checks understanding with each member of the group.

Step 4

The diagram is a means of analysis to show up duplication, ambiguities and inappropriate categorisation. Corrections are made.

Step 5

Team members are asked to identify the factors they perceive to be least significant. Depending on the total number generated 2, 3, 4 or 5 low priorities might be asked for. Those that receive the most 'votes' are deleted.

Step 6

Team members are asked to select the most significant factors (number to be determined by the total available) and to prioritise them. 'Votes' are again collected and the outcome recorded on the diagram.

The process has thus identified possible causes, categorised them, reviewed their relative significance and produced a prioritised list of causes.

Note that for some issues, and for large groups the diagram can be physically constricting. In this case Step 1 could take the following form:

Members of the group are asked to note down their contributions and the facilitator then goes round the group recording each contribution on flip chart paper and numbering it. The process is continued until all contributions have been recorded. The sheets of paper are displayed and Steps 3–6 of the technique are used in the same way.

This approach can also be used to generate and prioritise solutions to a problem, i.e. as a more sophisticated form of brainstorming. The topic is the problem to be solved and the team is asked to generate possible solutions which are in turn prioritised and reviewed.

This approach is a version of nominal group technique.

Five 'hows', five 'whys'

These are the same technique with a different focus. In both cases the idea is to explore a problem or solution until it is expressed in the simplest, most basic terms. In essence a team, with facilitator, examines 'how?' or 'why?' and each proposal is then subjected to further questioning until the root cause is felt to have been reached.

This technique can be exasperating and needs skilled facilitating but it is a powerful tool to overcome superficial responses.

Example

We need to extend the working life of textbooks.

How? 1

By encouraging children to take better care of them.

How? 2

By making them personally responsible for them.

How? 3

By introducing a better monitoring scheme.

How? 4

By designating someone as being responsible.

How? 5

By HOD reviewing job descriptions and negotiating the new responsibility.

Each stage of the process can generate a number of alternatives, each is followed through to the point where an individual accepts responsibility to act to produce a specific outcome within a specified timescale.

Forcefield analysis

Forcefield analysis helps a team to understand the context in which it is operating and to target factors working in its favour and those which are opposing change. FFA is derived from the premise that any change is subject to driving forces which will move it forward and restraining forces which will hinder. The technique can be used to analyse the existing situation, identify and build on strengths, identify and minimise restraints. FFA often centres around perceptions and feelings. However, as these can be the most important factors influencing behaviour in organisations they should be given high significance.

Step 1

The facilitator agrees with the group the topic to be analysed – this might be generated by brainstorming or the cause and effect process.

Step 2

Each member of the team is asked to work individually using the FFA sheet (Figure 9.2).

| IMPLEMENTING TEACHER APPRAISAL |

DRIVING FORCES		RESTRAINING FORCES
1.	LEGAL REQUIREMENT	➔◄	UNION CONCERNS
2.	BETTER INSET	➔◄	NO TIME
3.	IMPLEMENTING DEVELOPMENT PLAN	➔◄	LOW SKILLS
4.	BETTER QUALITY TEACHING	➔◄	TIME FOR TRAINING
5.	POSITIVE CLIMATE	➔◄	POOR RELATIONSHIPS
6.	RECOGNITION OF SUCCESS	➔◄	CONFIDENTIALITY
7.	CAREER MANAGEMENT	➔◄	NOT NEEDED
8.	BETTER MANAGEMENT	➔◄	NOT MY JOB

Figure 9.2 Forcefield analysis

Step 3

The facilitator manages the process of identifying, agreeing, prioritising and recording the team's perceptions. Several drafts of the team diagram may be necessary. Perceptions of the relative strength and significance of each topic can be indicated by the respective size of arrows placed on the continuum or listed according to priority.

Step 4

The team agrees on the driving forces to be reinforced and the restraining forces to be overcome. The two elements can often be correlated and a readiness and capability chart (see later in this chapter) used to target specific actions.

Measurement charts

This is a method of giving graphic representation of trends to facilitate analysis, identify non-conformance, create common understanding and measure change over time. This process can be used for a variety of purposes and helps to maximise the possibility of objective analysis. The process should not be seen as an attempt to quantify for its own sake but rather to help the process of measurement.

The first step is to identify an individual to be responsible for managing the process. According to the process to be measured, the criteria to be applied, the unit of measurement and the timescale to be used should all be agreed. In many school processes attaching numerical values may be problematic but in fact teachers are expert at translating children's work into grades and there is also considerable experience in the evaluation of INSET courses.

Let us take this as our working example: it has been decided to review senior management team meetings over a half-term period. The key components of a successful meeting are agreed and each team member completes the simple review sheet at the end of each meeting. The scores are aggregated and recorded and the reasons used as the basis for review, analysis and implementation of changes.

Senior management team meeting – review

Please rate each category below for this meeting. 1 = poor, unsatisfactory; 10 = excellent.

1	Agenda received in advance	1	2	3	4	5	6	7	8	9	10
2	Meeting kept to time	1	2	3	4	5	6	7	8	9	10
3	Documentation/data available	1	2	3	4	5	6	7	8	9	10
4	Decisions taken	1	2	3	4	5	6	7	8	9	10
5	Actions agreed	1	2	3	4	5	6	7	8	9	10
6	Full participation	1	2	3	4	5	6	7	8	9	10
7	Appropriate leadership	1	2	3	4	5	6	7	8	9	10
8	Planning and review sessions	1	2	3	4	5	6	7	8	9	10

A crucial decision is to establish a goal line: a standard which is regarded as the optimum to be achieved. For some processes this may be arbitrary but experience will identify proper levels.

The measurement chart for the team meeting could appear as in Figure 9.3. The chart displays relative satisfaction and provides a focus for analysis. Individual scores may be displayed as a means of generating discussion and involving all team members in the analysis of the factors leading to dissatisfaction.

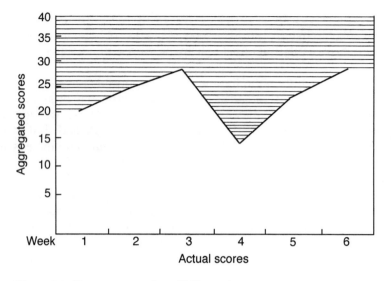

Figure 9.3 Measurement chart SMT meetings

This technique has the advantage of being simple and immediate; the discussion generated is more significant than the statistical validity of the method.

Pareto analysis

This technique helps to establish the vital elements of a problem from the relatively trivial. The approach is derived from the work of the Italian economist Pareto who put forward the '80/20' hypothesis, i.e. 80 per cent of the problems are caused by 20 per cent of the process. Pareto analysis is a means of identifying the real cause of the problem so that it can be addressed directly.

Step 1

Identify the problems to be compared by brainstorming or cause and effect analysis. Identify an appropriate unit of measurement and specify a time period for getting data.

Step 2

Gather results and display them using a histogram. Reorder the histogram so that it displays frequency declining from left to right.

Step 3

Label the right-hand vertical axis to show the cumulative percentage of the total distribution as in Figure 9.4.

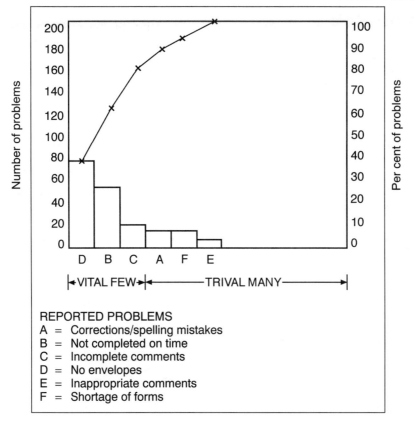

Figure 9.4 Pareto analysis of factors resulting in reports being sent out late

In the example shown in Figure 9.4 two factors account for two-thirds of the late reports. It is therefore possible to identify appropriate remedial activity which is specifically targeted. It also becomes possible to analyse the extent to which the problem has been overcome on future occasions. Although the result might be guessed intuitively the Pareto analysis ensures that the response meets the real need and provides evidence to ensure that future monitoring is effective. It also allows for a further stage of analysis to examine the factors causing the 'vital few' problems.

Problem-solving techniques

A rational, methodical approach to problem-solving increases the probability that the problem will be solved with the most appropriate solution. A diagnostic approach is more likely to result in high-quality outcomes. It is important to see problem-solving as a skill to be developed rather than depending on intuition.

The intuitive response starts from the recognition of the problem, tries to identify causes and then proposes solutions. The outcomes of this approach will include:

- solving the symptoms but not the problem;
- solving the problem but at high cost;
- solving the one problem but then creating others;
- not solving the problem or the symptoms but learning to live with both.

In a quality environment none of these outcomes is acceptable. The real problem must be solved (thereby removing the symptoms); the solution must not increase costs and must be capable of full implementation.

The components of a rational approach to problem-solving are shown in Figure 9.5.

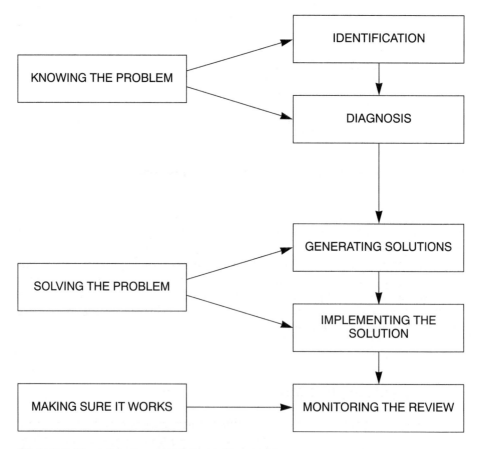

Figure 9.5 The rational approach to problem-solving

Components of problem-solving

Identification

This stage involves identifying the actual problem to be solved, i.e. not the symptoms but the core cause. In order to do this it is necessary to specify as many different aspects and components as possible. Techniques such as brainstorming, Pareto analysis, 'five whys' and cause and effect are appropriate at this stage. Once the problem has been identified it needs to be 'unpacked', i.e. to be defined further by distinguishing cause and effect. Pareto analysis and 'five whys' are appropriate here.

Diagnosis

Having identified the actual problem to be solved systematic analysis of the causes is then possible. Brainstorming and cause and effect analysis are appropriate. Once hypotheses have been developed they can be tested using measurement charts, Pareto analysis or active experimentation depending on the nature of the issue. At this stage it should be possible to identify the root cause.

Generating solutions

The first stage here is to generate as many solutions as possible – brainstorming is obviously a powerful technique in this context or nominal group techniques could be used; the 'five hows' may well be most appropriate. Once the options have been identified it is appropriate to employ team-based consensus decision-making techniques.

Implementation

Once the optimum solution has been identified it is vital to move swiftly to implementation. Forcefield analysis and readiness and capability are appropriate prerequisites to action. The actual solution should be expressed in terms similar to those concerned with delegation and effective teams – most importantly, setting targets specific to named individuals in a clear timescale with appropriate resources and authority.

Monitoring and review

Monitoring is necessary to ensure that the chosen solution is actually working. Immediate feedback will be obtained by using the same techniques that originally defined the problem. More specifically, measurement charts can be employed to allow generation of comparative data, interviewing those involved can also provide instant feedback. Longer term review is required for two reasons: first, to ensure that the solution is institutionalised, i.e. it becomes part of the way of working. Second, it is important to review the problem-solving process itself to ensure that it was cost effective and enhanced team skills.

Readiness and capability

The purpose of this activity is to analyse and increase understanding of the individuals involved in a process in terms of their:

- readiness, i.e. their motivation, capability commitment and willingness to be involved;
- capability, i.e. their knowledge, skills, influence and potential positive or negative power.

This is an individual activity but can usually also be carried out by a small team.

The individuals likely to be significant in a particular process are identified and their readiness and capability are then plotted (see Figure 9.6). On the basis of an individual's location on the grid it is possible to identify a range of strategies.

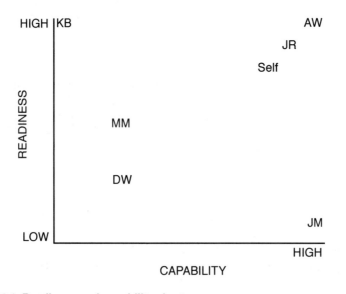

Figure 9.6 Readiness and capability chart
Note: initials refer to teachers involved

From the analysis shown in Figure 9.6 it is clear that AW is a significant person and should be fully involved from the outset. Those with high readiness and low capability clearly need support, development and training. Those with low readiness and high capability need to be involved and motivated to ensure that they do not become negative forces. The potential weakness of this approach (high subjectivity) can be overcome by sharing perceptions, e.g. by each member of the team completing the grid in respect of the other members and pooling and sharing perceptions. This will often facilitate openness about attitudes and can be a powerful team development activity.

Statistical methods

Readers are referred to Greenwood and Gaunt (1994) for the most detailed analysis and application of quantitative techniques to British schools. The central purpose of the use of statistical methods in total quality is to understand and so eliminate variation. Variation is the antithesis of quality as it implies deviation. The quality technique of Statistical Process Control (SPC) uses a range of standard statistical techniques to identify variations during a process and so facilitate corrective action to prevent failure at the final outcome.

Of course teachers will recognise this process – it is what most would argue to be the purpose of assessment. However, it is the way in which such data are managed that the total quality approach becomes distinctive. In this context quantitative data are:

- gathered in a consistent manner;
- processed and graphically presented;
- used as the basis for review;
- analysed to inform corrective action;
- used to benchmark standards;
- employed to determine success criteria.

Examples of the sorts of data that can be used in this way might include:

- attendance figures (pupils, teachers and parents);
- satisfaction ratings (see Chapter 3);
- course work assessment;
- value added calculations;
- external assessments, e.g. SATs, GCSE, A level;
- use of materials and resources;
- marketing strategies;
- equipment failure.

The combination of the vigour of SPC techniques with the use of graphical display could well transform normal patterns of assessment of pupils' work; however, as Greenwood and Gaunt (1994, p. 122) wisely point out:

One cautionary note should be added. Remember Deming's hatred of ranking and grading. Emphasise always to your students that they are not competing against each other, but collaborating to improve against some absolute standard.

Summary

- Managing quality is about measurement.
- All work is a process.
- Managing processes is about adding value.
- School processes can be measured.
- Prevention is better than inspection.
- Prevention is achieved through operating procedures.
- Improving quality means reducing costs.
- Quality is free.
- Techniques for improving processes are readily available.

Action

1 Analyse work processes in school and identify ways of improving them.

2 Identify examples of waste, calculate the cost and improve the process.

3 Start calculating the cost of non-conformance.

4 Start using the techniques for improving work processes.

5 Analyse your behaviour in terms of:
   - the clarity of the specifications you give;
   - the amount of 'hassle' in your life;
   - the amount of time spent reworking;
   - the amount of time spent dealing with problems, complaints and grievances.

10
■ ■ ■
Implementation

Introduction

This chapter outlines and discusses some of the issues associated with the implementation of total quality in a school. Four key issues need to be to the forefront of any implementation strategy:

1   'Just do it!' This was the reported response of Deming to repeated requests for advice on implementation. Although brief to the point of obscurity it contains a vital message: action is more important than analysis. There is a great danger of over-intellectualising the process.

2   A long-term view is needed; total quality is about attitudes and these are not moved by exhortation or lecture. In many organisations it has taken three to five years to be confident that a quality culture has been created. There are, however, very simple and direct actions that can be taken for immediate impact.

3   More organisations have failed to implement total quality than have successfully implemented it. The reason is usually a lack of commitment and a failure to appreciate the totality of the impact on an organisation. Piecemeal involvement is doomed.

4   The implementation process must be seen as a quality process in its own right. Those who are responsible for managing the implementation must use quality processes and techniques. The creditability of total quality will be determined by the sensitivity of its implementation.

This chapter will examine the principal components of the implementation process:

- leadership commitment;
- driving the process;
- review;
- strategy;

- training and development;
- structures and systems;
- management behaviour;
- continuous improvement.

Fundamental to these eight points is the management of change. It is not appropriate in this context to review all the issues associated with managing change, but two principles are worth stressing. Fullan (1982) argues that real change involves dealing with attitudes and values and therefore change has to be about learning. Joyce and Showers (1980) argue that real learning only takes place when a range of criteria is met – most importantly the notion of feedback on performance. Effective learning (and by extension, effective change) must therefore be firmly rooted in the work place and management relationships need to have development at their heart.

Leadership commitment

TQM will only work if there is explicit single-minded and obsessive commitment to quality. Any hint of compromise or reservation will diminish the credibility of the implementation strategy. The importance of vision in leadership has already been stressed; equally important is the way the vision is communicated and the way it is demonstrated in action.

Tribus (1994, p. 276) describes the introduction of quality strategies at Mt Edgecumbe stressing that from the outset:

> *purpose must be constant and not changing every day. It must be a purpose that attracts their hearts and minds. The students, the faculty and the administration spent considerable time developing a consensus about the purposes of the school.*

This agreement was possible because:

> *The students in these classes became co-managers of their education. The teachers became enablers, not task masters. Morale improved. Motivation improved. With the superintendent's enthusiastic support, TQM was launched (ibid.).*

The importance of leadership permeating the school is stressed by Murphy (1997, p. 136):

> *If the leadership is perceived… to be the sole preserve of the SMT, two problems can result. First the 90 per cent of staff who are not part of the SMT will, consciously or subconsciously, be less inclined to exercise leadership roles and second, the SMT are*

likely to be so stretched with management *tasks that they are unlikely to be able to devote sufficient time to leadership.*

Samuel (1997, p. 97) describes a different but equally valid and successful approach.

By now we had a Quality Committee. It comprised the four-strong senior Management Team (all the best books tell you that TQM is dead unless it has the active commitment of the leadership) and two other members of staff, one of whom was later to become the quality manager.

The specific requirements on leaders are clear:

- to develop and display consistency of purpose, i.e. to speak with one voice;
- to implement quality procedures in all aspects of their work – especially team development and problem-solving/decision-making techniques;
- to engage in training and development activities;
- to recognise that many quality problems are the result of management action;
- to ensure that resources are made available;
- to talk and act quality;
- to manage the implementation of total quality as a high priority.

In essence quality should not be merely an 'agenda item' but should permeate every issue. The question to be asked of every issue is: 'What are the quality implications of our response to this. . .?'

The chapters on leadership (7) and teams (8) have identified a range of skills appropriate to quality management. Long before senior managers presume to introduce TQM they should review their own preparedness and take appropriate action. The most important single determinant of the success of an implementation strategy is the behaviour of senior managers. Actions which are incompatible with the quality approach and language which implies scepticism or cynicism will inevitably diminish credibility and in turn create cynicism. Once initiated quality cannot be compartmentalised – it must permeate all aspects of school leadership and management.

Driving the process

Although quality is everyone's responsibility it is necessary to identify an individual and a team specifically responsible for driving the implementation process in the school. Commercial organisations usually appoint a total quality manager or facilitator. Schools cannot afford the luxury of a specific appointment but there is a need to designate a named individual to have responsibility for managing implementation. There are three criteria for such an appointment: authority to make decisions, knowledge of total quality, and enthusiasm and commitment. The specific responsibilities of such a post might include:

- promoting the total quality approach;
- acting as internal consultant to teams;
- advising managers on operational issues;
- designing and delivering training;
- liaising with external suppliers and customers;
- communicating progress to all staff;
- monitoring and evaluating the implementation process.

In essence the role of the facilitator is to make total quality live, to help all colleagues translate the theory into practice. However, the task is a major one and probably too much for one individual. It may therefore be appropriate to establish a quality team, a task team with the specific purpose of making total quality happen. Whatever the constitution of the team it should never be allowed to detract from the fact that every team has to be a quality team and the creation of a specific team should not allow others to abrogate responsibility for quality in their own sphere of activity. The existence of a 'quality team' can create inertia elsewhere.

The team's most appropriate functions are probably:

- to provide advice and support to the facilitator;
- to act as a model of effective team working;
- to integrate total quality with other school initiatives;
- to pilot specific strategies;
- to generate resources to support implementation;
- to act as a forum for generating commitment;
- to disseminate ideas and experience.

Two intangibles are vital to the quality facilitator and team: an infectious enthusiasm for quality and high levels of personal integrity.

The efficacy of this approach will be largely determined by the existing ways of working in the school. Samuel (1997) describes a highly successful method using the notion of a quality manager. The role was given three main foci. First was the operation of the quality system, in particular the continuous improvement of all procedures and processes in the school 'so that as soon as the possibility of an improvement can be described, it is put into action' (p. 99). Second was overseeing the review and development processes, in particular the school development plan and the compilation of management information statistics. Third the quality manager was responsible for managing the whole OFSTED process.

There is a debate as to the appropriateness of creating a distinct role for 'quality'. It could be argued that it might bureaucratise the process and lead to individuals seeing quality as someone else's responsibility. However in the early days of a profound change the existence of someone with enthusiasm, expertise and a specific remit more than compensates. As the quality process matures so it can be assimilated into every role and responsibility.

Review

In Chapter 1 review was established as a key link between total quality and the school effectiveness and improvement movements. Analysis of the current situation is the essential precursor to any quality initiative. Without a systematic review the strategy may be misdirected and become inappropriate, and more importantly key strengths may be ignored and thereby not integrated.

The main purpose of the review is to establish what is to be changed, i.e. to analyse the existing situation in quality terms. Such a review should be initiated and managed by the quality facilitator and might well follow the form of the inventory at the end of Chapter 1. The content and structure of the review should be determined by the context, audience and possible applications of the outcomes. Thus a range of review documents may be necessary, aimed at:

- children;
- parents;
- teaching and non-teaching staff;
- external agencies, e.g. the LEA, other schools etc.

Whatever the audience the same central issues remain:

- current levels of satisfaction;
- the extent to which needs are being met;
- how the school compares with other schools;
- identification of areas of waste;
- identification of areas of non-conformance;
- suggestions for improvement.

177

The results of this review process will help to identify the priorities to be taken into account in planning the strategy. The inventories can also be used at a later date to allow measurement of changes in levels of satisfaction, i.e. the extent to which the TQM process is actually changing the way the school is managed. Two important principles are established by the use of reviews: listening to customers at the very outset and measuring changing levels of satisfaction. The design of the review sheets should allow for quantification of results.

Stevens (1996) provides a compelling example of the systematic use of a review process:

> *The decision to use a more structured approach to solving problems and generating solutions was born out of a concern to apply the principles of TQM. Towards the end of the project I asked staff to complete an evaluation questionnaire about the work. The staff's response indicated that it had led to satisfaction in terms of outcome and the process. (p. 72)*

Review is the Achilles' heel of school management. It may well prove one of the most intractable areas in the real change of behaviour. Stevens describes a review process at the end of a project. This is a powerful strategy but in the total quality environment needs to be extended so that continuous review is implicit in every process. For example:

- annual review or audit prior to every planning cycle;
- systematic monitoring of key processes, e.g. learning and teaching, pupil behaviour;
- collaborative review of every lesson and meeting;
- regular testing of opinion, e.g. parents' consultation evenings, school meals etc.;
- detailed evaluation of major projects, e.g. the use of a literacy scheme, computer software etc.

There is, of course, a great danger that people will become 'tick sick', weary of completing questionnaires and survey forms. Review can take a wide range of forms often very simple. Two minutes at the end of a lesson will both give the children a voice and provide the teacher with instant feedback. Pupils and adults rapidly become adept at indicating a response using a range of evaluative criteria.

However, such an approach will not become endemic to the school unless the most fundamental management process, plan, act, review, is made implicit to every action – however quick and simple it might be. 'Review' needs to be on the agenda of every meeting.

PLAN ➤ ACT ➤ REVIEW

One cautionary note with the review process: once started it will raise expectations that will have to be met. Failure to act on the outcomes will almost certainly exacerbate existing concerns and create disillusionment.

Strategy

Once the personnel to manage implementation have been identified and priorities established it is appropriate to identify the specific strategy. Although the implementation of total quality has to be seen as a separate initiative it should not be divorced from school management processes. It should not be seen as a 'what?' but rather as a 'how?' It would therefore be appropriate to integrate the total quality strategy into the school development plan. The plan is necessary to provide a clear view of the path to be followed and to act as a quality criterion, a benchmark to monitor progress as well as a constant reminder of central purpose. The development plan needs to include: a mission statement; target setting; organisation; development and learning; resources; and criteria for success.

Mission statement

Existing school aims and 'objectives' need to be integrated into a mission statement as outlined in Chapter 5. The important change is in the language which should reflect the shift to customer satisfaction through quality processes. At this stage it is vital that the desired culture and values are made explicit and articulated into the mission statement.

Target setting

The mission statement should be translated into specific objectives which indicate the outcomes to be achieved in a specified timescale. These targets should have the following characteristics:

- success criteria are identified;
- timescale is specified;
- responsibility is delegated;
- resources are allocated;
- teams and individuals are specified.

These targets will form the basis of personal target setting. The targets should relate to the specific components of implementation, notably training and organisation. Target setting is seen as a powerful tool to enhance organisational and personal effectiveness in that it translates the complex and abstract into the specific and concrete. In the context of implementing total quality target setting is vital if pious aspiration and charismatic exhortations are to be avoided.

The process of review discussed earlier will be significantly enhanced if target setting becomes instinctive in every school process. Thus the school development plan is expressed as a series of whole school targets which can be translated as appropriate into departmental and individual targets. As with review it is vital that the process does not stop at the classroom door. Total quality requires that appropriate techniques are used by everyone in the school, thus pupils can use target setting to manage their work, as teachers do to manage lessons etc.

Organisation

The review will have indicated specific issues relating to the organisation of the school. Central to this will be the extent to which existing structures are compatible with the notion of quality teams. The plan should indicate the processes for transforming those structures and working procedures into vehicles suitable for managing quality.

Where appropriate there should be reconsideration of decision-making structures so as to facilitate the adoption of a quality approach. Murphy (1997) provides a number of powerful examples of change in organisational structure, deployment and role responsibilities in order to facilitate a change in organisational structure and culture. He describes how the role of form tutor has been given enhanced status and significance through the creation of a team approach.

- *The title of year tutor is chosen. ... Head of year implies a hierarchical approach.*
- *The year tutor is not given significantly more non-contact time than the form tutor; she/he may have less....*
- *The year tutor gains only one responsibility point – for the team leadership responsibility not for the pastoral responsibility.*
- *Teams of tutors with their team leaders stay together with their forms... from induction to congratulation!*
- *The year teams together form the tutorial faculty, so that most staff belong to two faculty teams. (p. 143)*

Development and learning

This is so central and significant that a move towards total quality cannot be contemplated without it. The issue is dealt with in more detail later but certain principles can be stated as fundamental:

- every stage of the implementation process should be accompanied by development;
- everyone should be developed;
- training should cover the spectrum of skills;
- the development programme should be based on a process of needs analysis.

The development plan should indicate the training priorities for implementing TQM, the methods of needs analysis to be employed, the means of delivery and the resources available.

Resources

The implementation strategy needs to be costed in terms of both financial expenditure and staff time. As with all educational activities many aspects of the management process will be difficult to cost. However, it is essential that an attempt is made in order to allow for prioritising in the budget and to demonstrate commitment.

It is also important to view expenditure on implementing TQM as an investment from which there may not be immediate returns. The most significant item of expenditure will be staff time, but the criterion to be applied here is that of opportunity cost – what will happen if significant change is not implemented? Most educational systems face a future of declining income in real terms. In this context it is very difficult to respond with anything but cynicism to Crosby's dictum that 'Quality is free'. Implementation of total quality will have costs associated with it – at the very least the costs of various quality assurance procedures which are externally validated. However, in formulating a strategic intent schools have to take into account year-on-year budgetary reductions with commensurate loss of flexibility. This is in a context of increasing demands – the classic 'more for less'.

Given this reality it may well be that the introduction of total quality approaches is the only way of enhancing what the school achieves while securing economies. Teachers cannot work any harder than they do: they are the central, crucial resource. It is therefore necessary to find ways of working smarter, of getting better value out of finite resources. Total quality techniques offer that potential.

Criteria for success

Integral to the development plan should be success criteria to allow progress to be measured. These should be as specific as possible and quantified where appropriate. One of the most important criteria will relate to the use of attitudinal surveys to measure the impact of the quality programme.

The success criteria should also relate to specific changes to be introduced and failure to meet targets should be examined using the tools identified in previous chapters.

Training and development

The success in implementing total quality depends on development because the success of the process depends fundamentally on attitudinal change. At the same time making the total quality approach work requires the application of very specific skills and procedures. Training has to be seen as an integral component of managing quality – it is not a parallel or even a support process but a fundamental component. Continuous improvement means continuous development and the principles of Right First Time and conformity to requirements are particularly appropriate. The following principles should apply:

- Training and development should be specific to the school and not 'off the shelf'; the language of training should grow out of the school's mission.
- Trainers, consultants and training materials should work to the specific needs of the school; customer needs must be stated.
- Training should not be restricted to attending courses or 'training days'; all meetings and activities should be examined for their training potential.
- Training activities should be designed to include feedback – coaching is an essential component to ensure that there is genuine change.

The training programme needs to include a wide range of topics, some specific to total quality, others of a broader applicability. The contents of a training strategy might include:

- introduction to the principles of total quality;
- identification of the need to change;
- raising the issue of customer awareness;
- analysis of work processes;
- application of quantitative and analytical techniques;
- team building skills;
- leadership skills;
- interpersonal skills, notably listening and feedback;
- oral and written communication and presentation skills;
- review and debriefing skills.

Many of these skills will already be present in schools, or will have been developed in other contexts; it is most important that extant skills are recognised and reinforced. Another very important issue is the training and awareness raising available to children, parents, governors and others who come into regular contact with the school. At the very least they need to be informed; at best a strategy will be developed to integrate them fully into the school's scheme.

One of the great potential strengths of total quality in schools is the development of the approach by children. They are clearly a vital source of feedback but also essential protagonists in making classrooms and schools quality environments. Most children have considerable skills in articulating their requirements; many adolescents are 'natural customers'. A school cannot claim to be a quality organisation unless all those with whom it comes into contact are integrated into quality processes and this includes training.

Training is too often regarded as a cost rather than an investment. One of the major problems is that training has direct costs (course fees, consultant charges etc.) and indirect costs (teachers not teaching, managers not managing). If the total quality approach is to be fully integrated into a school then training and development must be seen not as separate activities but natural components of all interactions. Departmental meetings become opportunities for team development – 'discussions' can be developed into coaching; everybody in a position of responsibility is expected to develop colleagues as an essential component of their job.

Any form of developmental process which is concerned with quality improvement should aspire to meet certain criteria. It should:

- focus on the core purpose of learning and teaching;
- be highly responsive;
- obtain high levels of involvement;
- integrate all stakeholders;
- set standards and measure progress against them.

In the context of the school it is vital that all development and training activities involving adults serve as a model, an exemplification of the very best practice aspired to in the classroom, laboratory, gym, studio etc. The effective learning of the individual should be a microcosm of the whole school approach.

Structures and systems

This is perhaps one of the most fundamental challenges to schools. Chapter 6 has identified the issues in terms of developing a quality structure and it would be wrong to underestimate the difficulties in changing a school's structure. The most significant difficulty is the inherited distribution of posts which cannot be abandoned overnight. Operating relationships and the concept of succession planning can be introduced to move the school's structure towards the desired format.

What can be done very rapidly is to enhance existing structures by refocusing and realigning their working procedures – in essence by converting departments into teams, by changing meetings into problem-solving and creative activities. This change can take place with minimal cost and disruption and can produce a dramatic impact on motivation, involvement and satisfaction.

More complex but equally vital is the realignment of systems. In practical terms this means establishing customer requirements and then recording them in such a way as to ensure consistency and conformity. This means producing codified operating procedures which define in significant detail the components of a process so there can be no ambiguity. Almost every aspect of a school's work is capable of being codified except the essential elements – what Handy (1990) refers to as the intangibles – and these cannot and must not be codified. It is not intended to advocate 'behaviour codes' requiring a standardised greeting with a regulation smile to greet thirty disaffected adolescents first thing on Monday mornings, even though many of those young people will themselves be subject to such a code on Saturdays at work.

What can be codified is the core of a process, the essentials. Examples of school activities appropriate to such an approach include:

- job descriptions;
- policies, especially relating to learning and teaching;
- syllabuses and schemes of work;
- procedures relating to attendance;
- review and reporting procedures;
- appraisal and staff development;
- marking criteria;
- homework procedures;
- uniform;
- health and safety;
- timetabling;
- record keeping;
- option procedures;
- records of achievement;
- development planning;
- budget planning;
- stock control.

Many of these activities are routine but all impact on customers and, if efficiently managed, can create time for more specifically educational activities – most importantly communication with children, parents and colleagues. It is only through codification that quality can be guaranteed – as long as it is customer requirements that are codified and not bureaucratic routines. Useful examples of the impact of policies on practice can be found in the study carried out by the National Commission for Education (1996); in essence:

> *'very little is left to chance'. Each of the successful schools endeavours to have a unified approach to the aims of the school. This often requires an explicit agreement among teachers about their aims and the implementation of policies and systems in many aspects of the life of the school....*
>
> *The sense of tight articulation between broad aims and operational procedures is evoked in... Burntwood School, whose ethos is described as a 'self-reinforcing system'. (p. 328)*

Schools undoubtedly benefit from clearer articulation of certain key functions. However, there is the danger that the system becomes all – the triumph of managerialism. It is through the culture of the school, the relationships and personal integrity that the most important qualities emerge: warmth, humour, creativity, excitement, love and a sense of personal value. These cannot be translated into a standard operating procedure, for which we all remain eternally grateful.

Management behaviour

The responsibilities of leadership have been discussed in Chapter 7. However, it is worth reiterating the importance of consistency during the implementation phase. If TQM is not to be dismissed as another management 'fad', as the result of another course or even the outcome of reading a book then certain attributes are essential.

Consistency

This means all managers, in all situations deliver the same message. The senior management team must speak with one voice and act with one purpose.

Enthusiasm

It is easy to ridicule the 'enthusiast' but real change will be directly proportionate to expressed commitment.

Attention to detail

Every aspect of work must be noted, successes reinforced and praised, problems solved and weaknesses and lapses picked up.

Listening

Listen constantly – always remember that we have two eyes, two ears and one mouth and that that ratio sends an important message to quality managers.

Accessibility

Be available, constantly on the ground, managing by walking about (MBWA).

In the final analysis quality management comes down to performance and relationships, and leaders have to display the highest standards of integrity in both at all times.

Continuous improvement

Although it is essential to have a clear strategy for the implementation of total quality it would be a mistake to see it as a separate process. It needs to be seen as the start of a process of continuous improvement in which there is continuous challenging of norms and expectations. Total quality implicitly denies the possibility that any organisation or individual has reached a plateau representing an acceptable level of performance. Implementing TQM requires the acceptance of the principle: 'We can always improve'. Although the gradient may lessen, going up is the only direction for a total quality school.

In practice this means constantly checking, redefining and improving. Schools are the most natural organisations for this culture as they are already expert in managing the most complex improvement process of all: the moral, intellectual, social and personal development of children.

Summary

■ Plan, act, review.

Action

1 'Just do it!'

Review

■　■　■

You, the reader, are my customer. In order to be consistent with the approaches advocated in this book, I need feedback from you. Would you therefore please complete and return the following review to me? Please ring the number that reflects your view.

1 The book met my expectations:
   Strongly disagree　　1　2　3　4　5　6　7　　　　Strongly agree

2 The book is relevant and practical:
   Strongly disagree　　1　2　3　4　5　6　7　　　　Strongly agree

3 The language and tone of the book are appropriate:
   Strongly disagree　　1　2　3　4　5　6　7　　　　Strongly agree

4 The structure and organisation of the book are helpful:
   Strongly disagree　　1　2　3　4　5　6　7　　　　Strongly agree

5 I can apply the strategies outlined in the book:
   Strongly disagree　　1　2　3　4　5　6　7　　　　Strongly agree

6 The book has helped develop my thinking about quality:
   Strongly disagree　　1　2　3　4　5　6　7　　　　Strongly agree

Any other comments on the book?

Any comments on the issue of quality in schools?

Thank you for your time. Please return this questionnaire to:

> John West-Burnham
> International Educational Leadership Centre
> Lincoln School of Management
> Lincoln University campus
> Brayford Pool
> Lincoln LN6 7TS

References and Bibliography

■ ■ ■

Adair, J. (1986) *Effective Teambuilding*, Aldershot: Gower.

Adair, J. (1988) *Developing Leaders: The Ten Key Principles*, Guildford: The Talbot Adair Press.

Adair, J. (1990) *The Challenge of Innovation*, Guildford: The Talbot Adair Press.

Atkinson, P.E. (1990) *Creating Culture Change: The Key to Successful Total Quality Management*, Kempston: IFS International Ltd.

Barker, H. and Bell, M. (1994) 'The National Standard of Investors in People – does it have a place in the management of schools?', in Green, H. (1994) op. cit.

Belbin, R.M. (1981) *Management Teams: Why They Succeed or Fail*, Oxford: Heinemann.

Belbin, M. (1993) *Team Roles at Work*, Oxford: Butterworth-Heinemann.

Blake, R.R. and Mouton, J.S. (1964) *The Managerial Grid*, Gulf Publishing Co.

Blake, R.R. and Mouton, J.S. (1978) *The New Managerial Grid*, Gulf Publishing Co.

Bone, D. and Griggs, R. (1989) *Quality at Work*, London: Kogan Page, Crisp Pub. Inc.

Bottery, M. (1994) *The Ethics of Educational Management*, London: Cassell.

Bracey, G. (1994) 'OCEA – The Oxford Consortium for Educational Achievement', *Quality and Learning*, **1(1)**.

Brown, A. (1990) *Customer Care Management*, Heinemann Professional Publishing Inc.

Byham, W.C. (with J. Cox) (1991) *Zapp! The Lightning of Empowerment*, London: Business Books Ltd, Random Century.

Caldwell, B.J. (1997) 'Global Trends and Expectations for the Further Reform of Schools', in Davies, B. and Ellison, L. (1997) op. cit.

Campbell, A. and Tawadey, K. (1990) *Mission and Business Philosophy: Winning Employee Commitment*, Oxford: Heinemann Professional Publishing Ltd.

Clutterbuck, D. and Crainer, S. (1990) *Makers of Management: Men and Women Who Changed the Business World*, Guild Publishing.

Collarbone, P. (1997) 'A Journey of a Thousand Miles . . . the Haggerston Journey', in Davies, B. and West-Burnham, J. (1997) op. cit.

Collard, R. (1989) *Total Quality: Success through People*, London: Institute of Personnel Management.

Covey, S. (1989) *Seven Habits of Highly Effective People*, London: Simon & Schuster.

Crosby, P.B. (1979) *Quality is Free*, McGraw Hill.

Crosby, P.B. (1986) *Quality without Tears: The Art of Hassle-free Management*, Singapore: McGraw Hill Book Co.

Dale, B.G. and Plunkett, J.J. (eds) (1990) *Managing Quality*, Philip Allan.

Davies, B. and Ellison, L. (1997) *School Leadership for the 21ˢᵗ Century*, London: Routledge.

Davies, B. and West-Burnham, J. (1997) *Reengineering and Total Quality in Schools*, London: Pitman.

Davies, B., Ellison, L., Osbourne, A. and West-Burnham, J. (1990) *Education Management for the 1990s*, Harlow: Longman Group UK Ltd.

Deming, W.E. (1986) *Out of the Crisis*, Massachusetts: MIT Center Advanced Engineering Study.

Department of Education and Science (1989) *School Teacher Appraisal: A National Framework*, Report of the National Steering Group, London: HMSO.

Department of Education and Science (1991) *School Teacher Appraisal*, Circular 12/91, London: HMSO.

Department of Trade and Industry (1984) *Standards, Quality and International Competitiveness*, Cmnd 8621, London: HMSO.

Doherty, G.D. (1994) (ed.) *Developing Quality Systems in Education*, London: Routledge.

Drucker, P.F. (1993) *Post-Capitalist Society*, New York: Harper.

Drucker, P.F. (1995) *Managing in a Time of Great Change*, Oxford: Butterworth-Heinemann.

Dyer, W.G. (1987) *Team Building: Issues and Alternatives*, 2nd edition, Addison-Wesley Pub.

Everard, B. and Morris, G. (1990) *Effective School Management*, 2nd edition, London: Paul Chapman Ltd.

Feigenbaum, A.V. (1987) *Total Quality Control*, Maidenhead: McGraw Hill.

Feynman, R.P. (1988) *What Do You Care What Other People Think?*, London: HarperCollins.

Fraser-Robinson, J. (with Mosscrop, P.) (1991) *Total Quality Marketing*, London: Kogan Page.

Fullan, M. (1982) *The Meaning of Educational Change*, Teachers College Press.

Fullan, M. (1985) 'Change Processes and Strategies at the Local Level', *Elementary School Journal*, **85(3)**.

Gardner, H. (1995) *Leading Minds*, New York: Basic Books.

Goldsmith, W. and Clutterbuck, D. (1984) *The Winning Streak*, George Weidenfeld & Nicholson.

Gray, J. and Starke, F. (1988) *Organisational Behaviour: Concepts and Applications*, 4th edition, Merrill.

Green, H. (1994) (ed.) *The School Management Handbook*, London: Kogan Page.

Greenwood, M.S. and Gaunt, H.J. (1994) *Total Quality Management for Schools*, London: Cassell.

Hall, V., MacKay, H. and Morgan, C. (1986) *Head Teachers at Work*, Buckingham: Open University Press.

Handy, C. (1989) *The Age of Unreason*, London: Arrow Business Books.

Handy, C. (1990) *Inside Organisations: 21 Ideas for Managers*, London: BBC Books.

Hannon, D. (1996) 'Preparing Student Teachers to Respond to Special Educational Needs', in Lomax, P. (1996) op. cit.

Hayes, R. and Abernathy, W.J. (1980) 'Managing Our Way to Economic Decline', *Harvard Business Review*, July/August.

Healy, M. (1994) 'BS5750 and Beyond in a Secondary School', in Parsons, C. (1994) op. cit.

Hendry, R. (1994) 'A Quest for Quality in Key Stage 1 Assessment', in Parsons, C. (1994) op. cit.

Hickman, C.R. (1991) and Silva, M.A. (1984) *Creating Excellence: Managing Corporate Culture Strategy and Change in the New Age*, George Allen & Unwin.

Hill, P. (1996) *Leadership for Effective Teaching*, Paper presented at the International Principals Institute, University of Southern California, July.

Hodson, P. (1987) 'Managers Can Be Taught but Leaders Have to Learn' *ICT*, November/December.

Honey, P. (1988) *Improve your People Skills*, London: Institute of Personnel Management.

Hopkins, D. (1987) *Improving the Quality of Schooling*, London: Falmer Press.

Horovitz, J. (1990) *How to Win Customer Service for a Competitive Edge*, London: Pitman.

Hutchins, D. (1990) *In Pursuit of Quality: Participative Techniques for Quality Improvement*, London: Pitman.

Ishikawa, K. (1976) *Guide to Quality Control*, Asian Productivity Organisation.

Jefferson, C. (1994) 'What do my customers want?', *Quality and Learning*, **1(1)**.

Jenkins, H.O. (1991) *Getting it Right: A Handbook for Successful School Leadership*, Oxford: Basil Blackwell.

Joyce, B. and Showers, B. (1980) 'Improving In-service Training', *Education Leadership*, **37**.

Juran, J.M. (1979) *Quality Control Handbook*, Maidenhead: McGraw Hill.

Kanter, R.M. (1984) *The Change Masters*, Allen & Unwin.

Kanter, R.M. (1989) *When Giants Learn to Dance*, London: Simon & Schuster.

Katzenbach, J. and Smith, D. (1993) *The Wisdom of Teams*, Boston: Harvard Business School Press.

Lessem, R. (1985) *The Roots of Excellence*, Fontana Paperbacks.

Lessem, R. (1991) *Total Quality Learning: Building a Learning Organisation*, Oxford: Basil Blackwell.

Likert, R. (1961) *New Patterns of Management*, Maidenhead: McGraw Hill.

Lomax, P. (1996) *Quality Management in Education*, London: Routledge.

MacDonald, J. and Piggott, J. (1990) *Global Quality: The New Management Culture*, London: Mercury.

McGregor, D. (1960) *The Human Side of Enterprise*, Maidenhead: McGraw Hill.

Martin, W.B. (1989) *Managing Quality Customer Service*, London: Kogan Page.

Mastenbroek, W. (ed.) (1991) *Managing for Quality in the Service Sector*, Oxford: Basil Blackwell.

Mohrman, S.A., Cohen, S.G. and Mohrman, A.M. (1995) *Designing Team-Based Organisations*, San Francisco: Jossey Bass.

Murgatroyd, S. (1985) 'Management Teams and the Promotion of Staff Well Being', *School Organisation*, **6(1)**.

Murphy, A. (1997) 'Leadership – for the Few, or for All?', in Davies, B. and West-Burnham, J. (1997) op. cit.

National Commission on Education (1996) *Success against the Odds*, London: Routledge.

Oakland, J.S. (1989) *Total Quality Management*, London: Heinemann Professional Publishing Ltd.

Office for Standards in Education (1995) *Evidence on the Inspection of Secondary Schools*, London: HMSO.

Parsons, C. (ed.) (1994) *Quality Improvement in Education*, London: David Fulton Publishers.

Peters, T. (1988) *Thriving on Chaos: Handbook for a Management Revolution*, Guild Publishing.

Peters, T. and Austin, N. (1985) *A Passion for Excellence*, Collins.

Peters, T.J. and Waterman, P. (1982) *In Search of Excellence*, Harper & Row.

Pinchot, G. and Pinchot, E. (1994) *The End of Bureaucracy and the Rise of the Intelligent Organisation*, San Francisco: Bennett Koehler.

Reynolds, D. and Stringfield, S. (1996) 'Failure Free Schooling is Clear for Take off', *Times Educational Supplement*, 19 January.

Royal Mail (1994) *Unit Excellence – The Self-assessment Handbook*, London: The Post Office.

Royal Mail (1995) *European Quality Award 1995 – Royal Mail Submission Document*, London: The Post Office.

Sallis, E. (1996) 'Total Quality Management and Further Education', Paper presented at the BEMAS Conference (1991).

Samuel, G. (1997) 'Introducing TQM at Heathland School', in Davies, B. and West-Burnham, J. (1997) op. cit.

Sawatzki, M. (1997) 'Leading and Managing Staff for High Performance', in Davies, B. and Ellison, L. (1997) op. cit.

Schon, D.A. (1983) *The Reflective Practitioner: How Professionals Think in Action*, New York: Basic Books.

Schonberger, R.J. (1990) *Building a Chain of Customers: Linking Business Functions to Create the World Class Company*, Guild Publishing.

Senge, P.M. (1990) *The Fifth Discipline*, New York: Doubleday.

Sergiovanni, T.J. (1992) *Moral Leadership: Getting to the Heart of School Improvement*, San Francisco: Jossey Bass.

Sieff, M. (1988) *Don't Ask the Price*, Fontana Paperbacks.

Sieff, M. (1991) *Management the Marks and Spencer Way*, Fontana Paperbacks.

Sisum, C. (1997) 'School Improvement – Translation from Theory into Practice', in Davies, B. and West-Burnham, J. (1997) op. cit.

Stevens, J. (1996) 'Focusing on Pupil Behaviour to Introduce Total Quality Management into a Middle School', in Lomax, P. (1996) op. cit.

Stewart, V. (1990) *The David Solution: How to Reclaim Power and Liberate your Organisation*, Crower.

Taguchi, G. (1981) *On-line Quality Control during Production*, Japanese Standards Association.

Taylor, S. and McKenzie, I. (1997) 'The Team Solution', in Davies, B and West-Burnham, J. (1997) op. cit.

Torrington, D., Weightman, J. and Johns, K. (1989) *The Reality of School Management*, Oxford: Basil Blackwell.

Tribus, M. (1994) 'The Application of Quality Management Principles in Education at Mt. Edgecombe High School', in Doherty, G. (1994) op. cit.

Trott, C. (1997) 'The Child as Client', in Davies, B. and West-Burnham, J. (1997) op. cit.

Tuckman, B.W. (1985) 'Development Sequence in Small Groups', *Psychological Bulletin*, **63**.

Webb, I. (1991) *Quest for Quality*, London: The Industrial Society.

West-Burnham, J. (1990) 'Human Resource Management', in Davies, B. *et al.* (op. cit).

Whiteley, R.C. (1991) *The Customer Driven Company: Moving from Talk to Action*, The Forum Corporation, Addison-Wesley.

Index

■ ■ ■